SUPER NATURAL COOKERY

SUPER NATURAL COOKERY

Recipes for Vegetarian Gourmets

Jim Corlett

Illustrations by Dave Colin

DAVID & CHARLES
Newton Abbot London Vancouver

0 7153 6737 4

Set in 10/13pt Univers Light and printed in
Great Britain by Ebenezer Baylis & Son Limited
for David & Charles (Holdings) Limited
South Devon House Newton Abbot Devon

Published in Canada by Douglas David & Charles Limited
3645 McKechnie Drive West Vancouver BC

For the Edwards Family, Tottenham
In memory of David

Pure men like pure food which gives true health,
balanced mentality, sustaining strength, life long
enough to search—pure food which has delicate
taste, soothes, nourishes, and brings them
joy—pure food that promotes the knowledge
of God.

Bhagavad Gita 17

ACKNOWLEDGEMENTS

David and Myre Edwards-May for their enthusiasm, and for their Scots and French backgrounds and families, especially Bill and Meg and Peter; The Berges and their Sigbjorn for Sigbjorn; L. M. Campbell for quiet avocados; Mary Lipovac for Croatia incarnate; Astrid and Erwin Grotzbach for Germanic and Bavarian goodies, and the Brandts, all members of the RSAA; Sonja Wagn for delicate arts; Lars for nutritional hints; Heather Eva for Cornwall; The House of Wick for holiday settings; The Ernest Martins, especially William who always knows a good melon, and what is more important, appreciates it, and for Devonia and spiritual support; J. Brit Pfann for 'wonderful'; Dennis Brown, jeweller for introductions; Jillian Jeacock for transport, London, and an educated palate (and metrics); Nigel Hockings for 'this is far out'; Emma Wood for saying 'yes'; Larry and Jonie and Minna and Mae and Kay and Dallas and Bennett and India; Dave and Maeve Colin, for illustrations, kitchen, Adam, Simon, licked and sucked by Seth and their vacuum Wurzel; And the typist extraordinaire, along with her hospitable husband and family, Sandra Skinner; And guests, present past and not present in body, but Soul.

CONTENTS

NEW WORDS

New words mean new concepts and so here's some natural mind expansion:

agar agar—gelatine made from red seaweed, sold as flakes or powder

alum—a hydrated double salt used in baking powder and for clarification

anise—an aromatic herbal seed, also the dried pods of the 'star' anise tree

Bing cherries—the dark wine coloured variety

blackstrap molasses—treacle-like 'mother liquid' from beet or cane distillation

carob—St. John's bread or bean, used in powdered form as 'chocolate'

collard—kale variation, rich in A, C, minerals

ester—flavour after alcohol is cooked

filo pastry—dry Greek pastry sheets

garbanzo flour—protein rich chickpea flour

gomasio—sesame seeds (toasted) ground with sea salt

macadamia nut—Australian dessert nut

miso—aged, thick soy bean sauce/paste

mung—Indian bean used in the Orient to germinate 'bean sprouts'

tahini—sesame seeds ground into paste

tekha powder—Japanese spice made from roots and aged soy paste

turbinado sugar—like demerara, a natural brown, unbleached sugar

vervain—verbena leaves used for tea

Yerba Mate (Yerba Sante, hierba del Paraguay)—a South American herbal tea

Zweibach crumbs—'twice baked' bread, somewhat like melba toast

LET'S BEGIN

Introductions introduce. So, Hello!

Then an apology if you thought this was a book of ghostly recipes requiring tsp (teaspoons) of wolfbane, or tbsp (tablespoons) of fungi gathered under full moons. What is intended by 'natural' is to lift off the coffin lid of unhealthy, starchy, polysaturated, franchised and chemicalized cookery. The 'super' is an attempt to avoid the other dark deed, those cauldrons of healthy but tasteless gop and smush that those in pursuit of the 'most' healthy conjure up for the good of the body and the austerity of the soul.

A quick example. From a nutrition viewpoint alone, white rice coated with vitamin B dust, and possibly milk powder, is capable of giving nourishment. Brown rice tastes better and may or may not provide protein enzymes that are polished off the white. But even brown rice is not a complete food, and so you will discover that the addition of herbs, nuts, a few soy beans, and fresh vegetable and fruit vitamins and minerals add health appeal, and rescue you from platefulls of dull chewing.

For I hope in this book to give you a foundation in sensible vegetarianism. Nutrition will be the primary concern as it is no good becoming sick on a diet intended to put you in the best of health. There will be quite a bit of concern for the amino acids (the building blocks of protein), vitamins and their retention through little cooking, minerals, and combinations and harmony of all the nutritional elements. Kelp (a type of seaweed) can be added to most foods for added minerals (especially the trace elements so essential for enzyme action) or can be taken in capsule form. It does much to balance out the rice discussed above.

The aesthetic side of this book is not only to promote the variety that keeps a diet interesting and free from fads, but is planned to give you bonuses in nutrition as well as taste. A few sprigs of parsley and you have your vitamin A for the day, and a few Brazil nuts will double your amino acids. But even though there is no particular value to a bit of fresh ginger, the zip it adds to a fresh tomato salad will empty the plate. It's time to end vegetarian zombiehood.

Aesthetic food does not mean that you will have to go beyond a decent fruit and vegetable shop, or chase to Ceylon for a piece of tamarind. All well if the exotic is available, but recipes using such ingredients are not much good if you are in the usual market town. This book does what it can to add a safe amount of the Continental and Oriental—a cheese sauce made with brown flour and herbed with lavender, does add protein as well as a memory of Southern France. Truffles if you will, but ordinary mushrooms are currently 57 times cheaper for the $\frac{1}{4}$lb!

There are a few exceptions to the above intentions, and they are those ingredients and occasional aids that may be best found at the local or nearby health food store. You may want as well to locate a supply of unsprayed

9

fruits and vegetables, and a mill that gives 100 per cent flour and not chalked flour. There are mail order firms (see Bibliography, p95) that you may find satisfactory and cheap. The various publications of vegetarian societies or *Seed* magazine can keep you advised on these matters. Spices and herbs are noticeably different if obtained from local gardens, or one of the firms that specializes in mailing out the whole leaves.

Time is of some value, so expect to find, that with the exception of some complicated dinner dish (such as the lasagne on p61), the whole time for preparation and cooking shouldn't take more than 30 minutes for even main dishes. Learning to do the salad while the rice is bubbling is an acquired skill, but many small pans and a sense of timing, mean a variety of dishes in a short time. Similarly bread, planned around other chores such as cleaning, or even marketing, can be created with no fuss. Besides, the smell of baking bread inspired whole generations of kids to faster furniture polishing.

Then, while ecology has become a fashionable word, fashion should not detract from its importance. Vast populations on a limited amount of land simply mean that care must be taken. My assumption is that you are the kind of person who doesn't want every tree converted into disposable wrapping for pre-packed vitaminless goop, the earth pillaged for and with tins, native populations robbed for yet more conveniences that they never wanted. So of course you carry a shopping bag and don't need paper, use fresh foods whenever possible and avoid foods that are grown by slave labour.

Natural food is for the environmentally conscious who want DDT-free foods, a diet suitable for our sedentary way of life, and that elusive feeling of being in harmony. So it is that this book will promote your learning to try lost arts such as apple tarts. For the process of discovering that ground grass seeds could make pastry and that pastry could cover fresh fruits, was an evolutionary process. But preserving and packaging the tart, and filling it with devious colouring, phony apples, non-digestible paste, saccharine, and an alphabet of embalming fluids is no progress at all. Leave the petrochemicals in the ground, let the trees grow, and save another apple orchard from caravan parking sites.

The social and ecological point of this book is to help make natural food such a delight and so easy to prepare, that resistance to these polluted non-foods can be strengthened.

Next it should be said that a number of observations have been gathered in much foreign travel and during culinary experiences with many different friends who live on a variety of diets. Fruititarians, macrobiotic meditators, vegans, living-off-the-woods friends, have all given this book a claim to some overview.

This is reflected in the presentation of some of the more common vegetables and grains in a variety of ways. Avocados (pp 18, 22, 42, 43) are the richest source of polyunsatured oils for the vegetarian, and soy beans whether sprouted or made into cheese (p67) or drunk as milk, or cooked (p56) supply beautiful amounts of protein. It seemed to be of more importance to use the easily available in a new way rather than dream up concoctions of exotica that no one eats but once in a lifetime.

That we are what we eat, that we think what we eat, that we have a life tied to what we eat—all this is easily seen. The business colleague who is used to too much wine and overly-lovely sauces does feel 'ten years younger' after a bit of drying out at an expensive health spa; another returns from a forced before-the-operation diet full of energy; heart patient friends learn to do with much less salt, fewer intoxicants, less cholesterol and no starched snacks; they all feel fine. Life can be lived free of pills and ills is what they learn, after the ills. This book is concerned with preventative measures. We need carbohydrates for energy, but not at the rate of four teaspoons of sugar in each cup of tea!

Finally, perhaps most importantly, along with our nutrional, aesthetical, ecological, and practical interests, we place the spiritual. The exploitation of animals as food fills them with hormones and chemicals, occupies a wasteful amount of space, subjects the feeling to factory techniques of production, and perverts kindness into cruelty—all of which are reasons for vegetarianism. It is the easing of one's conscience and the hope for further spiritual advancement that remain the soundest argument for vegetarianism. But this is a private matter, this escape from the feeling that one is earth bound, this freeing of oneself for meditation.

There should perhaps be the smallest words of caution. For the temptation once you begin to observe your diet is to observe it too much. Like legendary gourmets eating fried ant antennas, food then becomes an end in itself, and all too easily a religion—especially in this secular age. It is also possible to neglect proven aspects of nutrition, to give up all sources of vitamin C as one fad diet did, or to over-burden the kidneys with too much urea from overdoses of amino acids. There are intelligent texts about the needs of the human body, and while there remains much research to be done (especially in the area of vegetable protein, and the possibility that vegetarians synthesize some of their requirements) we are not living in such terrible ignorance as some would have you believe. Pill purveyors especially. To quote one sound nutritional guide: 'there is no nutritional advantage or benefit to health in having an intake above an individual's requirements of any nutrient.'

Finally a word about sensitivity. The world is sometimes not, and being a vegetarian has its trying moments. But tolerance is appreciably increased if you will inform hosts (including major airlines) of your particular diet. Be prepared for boo-boos, the beef stock potato soup, the potato salad with eggs and prawns. Smile, and quietly diet. Don't be forced into eating what you know will make you ill, but being unkind to humans is forgetting that they too are fellow animals. It is often wise to take the initiative by having your friends to a vegetarian meal first.

FOODS IN SEASON

Our seasonal symbols will be found throughout the book to indicate when fresh foods are available.

Spring

Summer

Autumn/Fall

Winter

ABBREVIATIONS

tablespoon	— tbsp	gram	— g
teaspoon	— tsp	kilogram	— kg
ounce	— oz	litre	— l
pound	— lb	millilitre	— ml
pint	— pt	centimetre	— cm
inch	— in		
minute	— min		

MEASURES

Metric approximates as used:

1oz — 30g
1lb — 500g
2pt — 1l

USA

For the benefit of US readers, where British and American measures differ we have given approximate equivalents. We have tried to use a language common to both countries and, where words differ, have always 'translated' for both sides of the Atlantic! For the purposes of this book the tbsp measure is the same amount for both UK and US cooks.

NB: Imperial measures are always given first— metric, then US follow in brackets.

HERBS

First things first. There are those who use no herbs or spices, but the parsley, sage, rosemary and thyme illustrated above are respectively a rich source of vitamin A; a way to make even stale bread crumbs palatable as sage dressing (just a spoonful per cup of crumbs, and water from the vegetables to moisten); an enhancer of pears or a superb oil for a rosemary shampoo; and the last, thyme, is that secret ingredient that Italian chefs use to turn tomato paste from red to a delicate golden brown, and bully the cooked onions into docility. The list goes on as you can see overleaf. But there is only one way to learn about herbs. You must try them all, and with as large a variety of dishes as you can. We can share in our experiments, but I suggest that you keep a file on your herbal adventures just as connoisseurs keep track of particular vintages. You will then settle your own tastes yourself, by taking a little time to record your findings. I, for instance, have never found oregano to be interesting in tomato sauce, and have always preferred basil and, as mentioned above, thyme. Then, I like coriander, a member of the carrot family, and nutmeg, in English cheeses, whereas a friend hates nutmeg and wants more of coriander. The illustrator of this book can work his nutmeg grinder all day, and still want more on the beetroot borsht on p19. But preferences as they may be, a large acquaintance with fresh herbs is essential to keep the same dish interesting year after year. Anything you do all day is related to the relaxation of the meals that day, and eternal sameness in saltiness affects you as certainly as monotony of motorways and identical architecture.

Do grow your own, even a few in a flower pot will make a bed-sit livelier, and a jar of parsley will provide 8mg of carotene and

150mg of ascorbic acid per gram, or twice or more of the daily requirements, the chlorophyll in the leaves sometimes being so intense as to raise even these figures 50 times.

This book will suggest herbs all along the way, not dogmatically, but just as teasers to the palate. Give us a chance, reject a particular herb if you wish, but do not reject herbs themselves. Rare herbs from the far East, the leaf of a certain tree in Borneo, and so on—these are for your advanced collection. Do keep the fun in perspective with questions such as food value. Vegetarians do well to consider yeast as a herb by way of getting valuable B-complex vitamins (see p 20). The following is an ideal beginner's collection: alfalfa seeds for tea and sprouts, allspice, anise, angelica, balm, bergamot, basil, borage, burdock, burnet, caraway seeds, cardamom for Indian delicacy, celery seeds and leaves, chervil, chamomile, cinnamon in sticks and powder, cloves whole and ground, coltsfoot, comfrey for B12, coriander, costmary, cumin, dandelion roots for coffee, dill, elder flowers, fennel, garlic, ginger, golden seal, hyssop, lavender, lemon and lime peel, lime flowers, liquorice, lovage, mace, marigold, marjoram, mint, nutmeg, oregano, paprika, parsley, pennyroyal, peppermint for soothing tea, purslane, rosemary, rose hips, rue, saffron, sage, sarsparilla, sassafras, savoury (winter and summer), sorrel, southern wood (rare), tansy, tarragon, thyme, vanilla, violet, and bitter wormwood. Sea salt and red, white and black peppers, blended curries, and there you are. We'll introduce you to as many as we can as we go along. Meanwhile better liberate those bottles.

LES HORS D'OEUVRES

You can buy volumes on all those delightful little titbits that stall the guests while something cooks, or keep the cook from temper if guests come late. The wish is not to serve some vapid pasty nothing, or to ruin appetites—a nice tug of war. So, here are some ideas tested and true:

Feta Cheese

This gift of the Greek goats (or sheep) is so solid that it can be fried lightly in olive oil, garnished with capers and black olives and used to recreate Homeric simplicity.

Litchi Nuts

Pit the fresh ones (points to you if you find them) and fill the cavity with stoned cherries or fresh raspberries. (Tinned ones will do.)

Melon Boats

Any full ripe melon (as well as feeling the end, smell it for melon aroma) cut into quarters or eights (if a big casaba) can be deseeded and turned into a flotilla. Use a sharp knife to completely separate the melon and the skin. Then make small cross-length slices and pull away from the centre in a right-left pattern to make 'oars'. Make a sail from a wedge of orange peel, light a birthday candle for a rudder, and launch your party with a Venetian night festival.

Mandarin Oranges

Slit the segments to make envelopes around seedless grapes, held in place with piped cream cheese.

Dates

Replace the seed with a Brazil nut and dip into whipped-until-smooth boursin cheese from France. Be prepared to slap greedy hands that reach more often than others . . . probably your own.

Gjetost

Buy some of this Norwegian cheese and use a cheese knife to pare on to waiting Swedish rye wafers.

Papadoms

Available from some large stores that have Indian goods or at a nearby Indian emporium. Fry for just seconds in several inches of hot oil.

Trays

Collect pickled miniature corn-on-the-cobs, Syrian bread spread with sesame tahini, blue cheeses stuffed into nectarines, salted wedges of turnip, various kinds of olives dried in oil, Italian pickled carrots, nut butters wrapped in steamed grapevine leaves, giant figs filled with sunflower seeds, or pumpkin kernels, and arrange so as to entice and nourish.

SOUP SENSE

Cups and bowls of soup are usually just for decoration in the non-vegetarian household, but here they will be presented from another viewpoint entirely—that is, as full meals in themselves. Food values have been worked out as well as the taste. An example is the vichyssoise that we prepare with dried yeast flakes, or the three lentil soups with their protein complements. Yeast for the B-complex family, potatoes for their vitamin C (more on this later) and lentils for calcium. And so on it goes: the chili is full of bean power, the pea rich in amino acids, the cheese in the fruit soups matches the protein in the nuts, and the borsht restores lost minerals. So it is that it is best to chew these soups and not just gulp them down. If the vital salivation takes place, you will gain far more food value. Finally, please do not boil soups, bubble them. Keep the heat down, and the vegetables fresh. If you want a particular dried herb flavour, first make an infusion of the herb and the water. Croutons (diced bread crumbs lightly fried in butter or oil) add fun to serving. Use left over pot liquor (water from vegetables), water from pasta cooking or gluten making, or juice from the juicer along with vegex cubes for extra richness. Milk adds calcium and phosphorus as well as protein.

Cauliflower Soup Chantilly

They (oh yes, those third person plural nobodies that nobody knows) make, or better yet concoct, a dried califlower soup. Dyed wall-paper paste probably tastes better! Not that our intent is to be negative. On the contrary, it's just a way of saying that some of 'their' dried, frozen or tinned soups are no easier to prepare than the following—which is but one of many if you read on:

Serves 4

Simmer 1pt (½l, 2½ cups) water with pinch tarragon and one bay leaf, while washing a medium firm white to light yellow cauliflower (with its green leaves, and stalk) being careful to cut out brown or soggy spots. Separate the fronds, and wash again. Then cut across the top of each frond so that you get round Chantilly lace sections. Cut up two carrots for colour and vitamin A, and a medium beet (for phantasy hues) and put all pieces into the water. Turn off the heat. After five minutes, sample one bit of carrot to see if crunchily cooked. If not, you may need to turn stove back on. Do not boil. To serve, add sour cream, dash of nutmeg, bits of soft cheese, or chives.

So there you have it, fortification with an aesthetic experience!

David's Vermicelli Broth

Families in rural France start most of their meals with a bouillon of some kind. Although the best known is the pot au feu, a vegetable broth is made just as often from a few potatoes, leeks, onions and carrots. The vegetables are finely cut and cooked gently in lightly salted water (sea salt to be sure). When the vegetables are cooked they are puréed in a blender or put through a sieve, and then returned to the water. A handful (2-3oz, 60g) of vermicelli per person is then added and the soup simmers for another 5 or 10 min.

Carrot and Leek Soup

The carrots are fresh from the garden, the leeks just washed and clean. The drama—a mild Chinese one—begins. Cook the cross-sliced carrots (several per person) until just tender in a small amount of water with $\frac{1}{2}$ tsp of basil for each serving. In another pan, cook the leeks, cut up, in a mixture of milk and water and a dash of mace, or freshly ground nutmeg. In a skillet, melt a bit of margarine or butter, then sprinkle in whole wheat flour and stir rapidly. When crisp and bubbly, pour in sufficient water from the carrots to make a thick gravy. Keep stirring and then add the leeks and their water. Keep stirring (what a good use for the proverbial wooden spoon) until the bubbling becomes a gurgling, then add carrots and remaining water. Thin if necessary with a bit of milk, and there you are. The double plots have merged, the climax has been reached, and you have but to collect the applause.

Darker variation: It is quite an elegant treat to braise a handful of fresh mushrooms in butter and use in place of, or in addition to, the carrots. Pure sylvan drama if you know what you're doing out in the woods at mushroom time.

Lentil and Cream Cheese Soup

Here's a quick hearty one. Using 1 handful per serving of the smallest red lentils (or dahl, the Indian version) bring to boil in $\frac{1}{2}$pt (300cc, $1\frac{1}{4}$ cups) water with 1 good tsp of tarragon (unless you have the Indian methi leaves). Turn the heat down and cook gently for 10-15 min, or until the lentils are soft. Remove from heat, and whip in $\frac{1}{4}$lb (125g) of plain cream cheese, or cream cheese with cucumbers cut in. Serve in bowls with much parsley (pulled apart) for your vitamin A.

Lentil, Carrot and Soy Soup

As above, only the carrots should be added about half way through. They should not be overcooked, even if mother did! Then where the cream cheese comes in above, add a can of soy meat substitute, soy grits, or a cup of soy beans that have been precooked. This is a good soup to use as a base for emptying out all those bowls of left-over goodies in the icebox and such cheese bits as you have collected in the cheese box.

Lentil Tomato Soup

As above for the lentils, but stir in freshly-sliced tomatoes (2 per person) or, in the winter when prices get ridiculous, a small can, or good squeeze, from a tube of tomato paste. Maybe a bit of fried onion? Garlic if you are so inclined.

Pea Soup

4pt (2·5l, 10 cups) water
2lb (1kg, 5 cups) fresh garden peas (shelled)
1 large sweet onion
1 sprig parsley
1 tbsp butter
pinch tarragon
few mint leaves

Cook the peas along with the chopped onion and other ingredients until tender. Add herbs sparingly, otherwise you will detract from the delicate flavour of the peas. Pass through a sieve or a ricer. (You may wish to leave some of the peas whole, as this adds texture to the soup.) Reheat, stir in butter, and serve with croutons (see page 15) or toast.

Parsnip-Carrot-Endive Lettuce Soup

It's late in the year, and the garden (hopefully you have one, or access to a good fresh vegetable farm) has only the last parsnips and carrots, and the endive lettuce (the kind with all the curls) is running to seed—Ah soup time! In a large pot, put 1qt (1·25l, 5 cups) of soup stock or herbed water and bring to boil with additional fresh basil. Cut up 5 parsnips, 5 carrots, and simmer for 10 min. Add one bunch of endive lettuce cut into wide strips. Cook for an addition 2-4 min, and serve. The tiny spinach pasta normally used for perking up the diets of Italian bambinos is a delicious addition.

La Sopa del Aguacate

Per serving:

Take one avocado, firm to ripe, cut open and remove seed. Scoop out pulp and smash tenderly! Put aside. Heat ½pt (285ml, 1¼ cups) creamy milk with a tip of tsp of cumin or several dashes of nutmeg. Add bits of red and green dried peppers or, if you want the olé, red or green chilis. Please be careful with chili, a little does more than you may desire by way of setting off a blazing fire. Then add a pinch of sea salt, and chives if they are about. Bring the liquid almost to the boil (in other words don't scorch the milk). Remove from the heat, and fold in the avocado pulp. Return to the fire just for simmering. Serve with dashes of paprika, croutons of whole wheat bread, and a lump of butter.

Winter happiness, cool summer evening joy.

Borsht

There are multitudinous varieties of this soup or stew but one of the easiest to prepare is this:
Cut 1 medium sized beetroot into cubes (per serving). Cook in the smallest amount of water that will keep from burning. When soft, and water evaporated or absorbed, add 4 or 5 tbsp yogurt per beet. Grind fresh nutmeg all over, and serve with lots of fresh cress as a topping. A slice of fresh lime is luxury.

Beet Croquettes

Not a soup, but another beet dish and a quickie. When talking about the past, a kind Polish gentleman suddenly remembered a childhood meal of chopped up, cooked beetroot, moulded and fried, and held together with bits of bread, the flour from bread-making, and a ground-up piece of old cheese with a little water or sour milk to keep it all moist. Fried on a hot oiled frying pan (skillet). Served with *kasha* (see p47).

Chili con Queso

Chili, its Spanish name reflects the peppery origins of this Texas dish, can be a soup or stew (depending upon your addition of liquid) but is best thick. One version of its origin is that a Wild West sheriff had beans, catsup, some bad buffalo, and worthless prisoners, but this recipe is purity itself.

Per serving:

4oz (125g, 1 cup) cooked kidney beans, from a
tin, or freshly cooked (if you use dried beans
then give them an overnight soaking, followed
by cooking until soft)
handful whole wheat bread crumbs or soy grits
or meat substitute
1 small tin tomato paste (2oz, 60g)
1 tsp cumin seed
½ tsp basil
red chili powder to taste (say ½ tsp)
4oz (125g) cottage cheese
1 medium sized onion, diced

Cook in a pot at medium heat (tradition says nicely blackened cast iron pot, over an open fire) for 10-15 min (not the traditional half day) and that's it. Milk may be added for a creamy texture, and also for slight thinning and pourability.

Yeasty Vichyssoise

This calls for the confession that I have never liked to put dried yeast into dishes, even though I have long known that it was a cheap form of the best amino acids and a goldmine of the B-complex family (so essential for the vegetarian). Other than on the Cursio's salad (p28) I have had to force it into my diet. Until, in the course of wondering how to add to that vitamin C source, the potato, I hit upon the following super-good vichyssoise. Hot or cold, of course, and quick, and cheap.

Per serving:

1 medium sized potato
2 cleaned leeks, in 1in (2·5cm) sections
1 carrot (optional)
ground sage and tarragon to taste
4 fl oz (115ml, ½ cup) water
parmesan cheese
2 heaped tbsp dried yeast
4 fl oz (115ml, ½ cup) milk
fresh parsley or mint or chives

Cook potato(es) in water with spices until soft (8-12 min), remove and dice with skins. Return to water and add leeks, carrot, and spices. Whip in parmesan, yeast and milk, and top with fresh herbs. Aim for a reasonably smooth texture. Serve hot, or chill.

Fruit and Nut Super Soups—Hot or Cold

This soup is always different and always good. As it will be up to you to settle on your own set of variations, only the structure will be given.

Per serving:

(1) 1 cup fresh fruit (apricots)
(2) 4oz (125g) cream cheese (pineapple)
(3) chopped nuts (5 or 6 Brazil nuts)
(4) dried (6 dates) or fresh fruit
dash of spice: nutmeg, cinnamon, mace, cloves, allspice, or even homemade curry

Mix together in a pan and heat with sufficient water 4 fl oz (115ml, $\frac{1}{2}$ cup) to make soupy. DON'T BOIL. Cooking time at most 5 min.
Notes: If tinned fruits can be used, especially pears or apricots which don't lose nutrition through canning, less water will be needed. Other alternatives:

1 Plums, pears, apples, or for exotic taste, fresh papaya. I have also used peeled Chinese gooseberries (Kiwi Fruit), Jack Fruit, grapes (the seedless variety), stoned cherries and once, and only once, crab apples.
2 Yogurt, ricotta cheese, cottage cheese, and over-ripe Camembert cheese.
3 Any nut — cobnuts, peanuts, pistachios, cashews, pinolas, or even spoonfuls of nut butters.
4 Figs, dried peaches, pears, apricots (the un-sulphured types, please), and dried bananas.

This dish can be a dessert, but I find it makes a quick working lunch, or a starter for a cheese pasta dish.

Rommegrot

This dish was lovingly prepared last summer by the aunt of a friend, and served with much cinnamon, brown sugar, and happy festivity (and isn't the joy of a well-prepared meal what makes it special? The ingredients couldn't be plainer):

Bring 16 fl oz (455ml, 2 cups) sour cream to a rolling boil for 5 min. Sprinkle in 4 tbsp unbleached white flour, and be prepared to whip the mixture until butter oozes out at the top. Skim butter off and reserve for later. To the bubbling mixture, now add more flour, about 3oz (90g, $\frac{3}{4}$ cup) then thin with $1\frac{3}{4}$pt (1l, $4\frac{1}{2}$ cups) milk. Boil for at least another 5 min, stirring all the while to obtain a smooth velvety mixture. Add sea salt if desired. Makes enough for 4 generous soup bowls topped with the reserved butter, spice and brown sugar.

SALADS

Salad Dressings

The British response to fashion is quick or even inventive. However the dressings available for salads are unhappily dowdy and frumpy: eggy salad creams and harsh vinegars and rancid oils. Please, oh please, toss them out and not on to some innocent lettuce!

Use instead, proper tarragoned vinegar, the light fresh oils of safflowers, sunflowers, green olives (an early pressing), and fresh herbs and cream. Please, proper cheeses and not processed plastics. And stop wiping the bowl with endless garlics, it's ruining the bowl. Criticism is over—on to creativity.

Try ½ a slivered beetroot mixed into 8 tbsp of fresh cream, garnished with a handful of cress and made piquant with a squeeze of fresh lime—on a bed of lettuce.

Or: 2 vegetable bouillon cubes crumbled into 5 tbsp of sunflower oil and garnished with chopped chives—on curly endive.

Or: tarragon and dried mustard by the tsp mixed into tbsp of milk, 1-2 tsp honey, a good splash of natural cider vinegar and green olive oil, to mix up piquancy for raw cauliflower fronds or sweet and sour broccoli pickles (refrigerate 24 hr).

Or: chopped pitted fresh cherries mixed in a carton of fresh yogurt, and poured over slices of apple and pear for pink madness.

Or: cucumber grated into sour cream, and spread over protein-rich Swedish rye crisps (with sprinkles of caraway seeds).

Or: 1 avocado scooped out of its shell and whipped into a purée, with 2 tbsp of yogurt and a dash of cumin powder for a super dressing on lettuce, and one sectioned and seeded grapefruit.

Hearts of Artichokes

One jarred or tinned vegetable that can be kept for drop-in guests, or that night following a day you missed the market is artichoke hearts. Lovely with a bit of lemon, 1 tsp or so of fresh cream, a little olive oil (unless preserved in oil) and such green herbs and cheese bits as you have. Perfect for after the theatre served with whole-meal biscuits and cream cheese. Heated in a thin white sauce (milk, flour, butter) artichoke hearts can even become a soup. Salad or soup, the guests will purr.

Cooked Beetroot Salad

You can, to be sure, begin this one by cooking your own beetroots, but if your greengrocer has acquired a reputation with you for whole-some vegetables, then you may want to speed things up a bit, by buying cooked beets. It is essential, however, that they are not vinegared, and preferable that the skins are not yet peeled off. A cheese wire is useful, though a knife will do, to cut the beet into small cubes. Then in the salad bowl, sprinkle on powdered cloves or a bit of freshly ground ginger. Pour on sufficient cream, or sour cream to cover, and allow to turn into a soft velvet colour. Add bits of grated carrot for additional eye-appeal or fresh mustard cress for zip. Simplicity. Great to eat with a stuffed baked potato.

Cranberry Salad

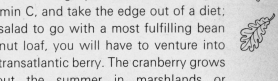

For a salad to charge your batteries, load you with vitamin C, and take the edge out of a diet; or for a salad to go with a most fulfilling bean stew or nut loaf, you will have to venture into eating a transatlantic berry. The cranberry grows throughout the summer in marshlands or cranberry bogs and absorbs a sunny brightness combined with fresh watery coolness. The salad is preferably made with a packet of the fresh berries, usually available in November and December, though tins of whole berry sauce are quite acceptable. Put fresh berries in a sink of lukewarm water, and check care-fully any that sink, for bad spots and discard. You may want to repeat this process again with fresh water. Use a coarse blade on your vegetable grinder to mince the drained berries, or a sharp chopping knife. Collect the bits in a bowl then grate orange peel and almonds over the whole. Spice with dashes of clove or allspice and, if you want to soften the tang, pour cream mixed with honey on as a dressing. Decorate with clemantine slices. The salad can be put into a gelatine if lightly cooked for a few minutes. Powerful.

GELATINES

Gelatines are infrequently seen as salads outside of California, and yet their very blandness allows them to be the base, not only of tomato aspics but all variety of salad 'coolers' in different-shaped moulds. Vegetarians must be careful to obtain gelatines made from Irish moss or sea-weed as the normal supermarket variety contain all the parts of animals between the meat and the squeak. You may want to concoct your own flavours as even varieties in health food stores are dyed and artificially flavoured. Dieters may like to try a gelatine with shredded carrots, green pepper, cabbage and cottage cheese; one with bean sprouts, celery bits and clementine oranges (deseeded); white seedless grapes and apple. Those non-dieters will want to add cashews, walnuts, Brazil nuts, and hazel nuts to the above, and even bits of apricot, peaches, a jar of Morello cherries, a can of lychees, or figs and dates. A pastry tube of cream cheese decorates. Use blackcurrant juice along with the water, juice of limes or lemons, but avoid raw pineapple — it inhibits the jelling. For a most decorative salad from California, whip cream into the almost-set gelatine, then fold in orange sections, wedges of peeled avocado and strips of pimento (see p90). Palm and artichoke hearts put into wild patterns, and held in place with piped on cream cheese mixed with puréed avocado. Gorgeous.

Fruit Jelly or Gelatine

It is possible to make your own gelatines, and it can be done as set out here:

Soften 3 tsp of agar agar in ½pt cold water for 10 min, stirring once or twice to make sure that all has dissolved. Bring 1pt (570cc, 2-2½ cups) strained berry juices to a boil, adding the agar agar and letting boil for 1 min, keeping the whole in motion by constant stirring. Add such fruits as you wish (but not bananas—they will cook—or, as mentioned above, pineapple); cool mixture, then put into a mould. Put in a coolish place to gel overnight, or in the coldest part of the refrigerator if in a hurry.

Carrot Salads

Carrots—young tender ones which have some sweetness—are a simple salad base once grated. Mix with seeded raisins, sultanas, red, black or white currants and orange slices dressed with a bit of honey and yogurt. Loverly, as Liza said. Or, make a spicy blend of carrots and cress, especially the peppery water-cress, dressed in ½ tsp mustard, curry powder and ginger, in 8 tbsp sour cream.

Vegetable Salad Plates

Rather dull—those ground veggies that end up on plates, even at vegetarian restaurants. Pity, since just a small grater can cut up beauty and flavour if you work at it. Arrange the following into sunflowers, with or without the suggested condiment as you wish:

fresh swede or turnip (a dash of soy sauce);
carrot (dusted with ground cloves, cardamom);
peppers (with ground ginger);
sweet onion (with curry powder);
parsnip (with nutmeg);
cucumber (caraway seeds);
cheese (coriander);
beetroot (anise seeds);
lightly cooked asparagas (mustard);
celery (poppy seeds);
black or red radish (caraway seeds);
raw or lightly cooked mushrooms (dill);
lightly cooked green beans (basil); peas (marjoram); sweet corn (borage) or any of the cabbage family.

Serve with bowls of yogurt, garnish with cress, watercress, lettuces, spinach, or cooked greens, say, Chinese cabbage, and complement with a good pumpernickle or rye bread and a glass of juice. Mix and match with fruits as well.

Fruit Salad Plates

Salads of fruits are not acid oranges, desiccated (and dead) coconut and dyed cherries, or an overcooked peach on a cardboard cottage cheese. Aren't you glad!

What they are is up to your taste buds, but here are a few suggestions for mixing:

grapefruit sections with white grapes and mandarin oranges with a sprinkling of mace;
fresh pears under mounds of pitted cherries;
apricots and slices of papayas and cubes of pineapple;
blueberries mixed with apples and yogurt;
strawberries and peaches cut together;
the fruits mentioned on the next page, those exotic fruits in combinations such as Chinese gooseberries peeled and sliced with melon;
or soft desert cheeses melted over a fresh fruit;
or all of them mixed as you wish.

Grapefruit turns all rosy in the company of beetroot cubes, cabbage salads enjoy bananas and raisins in a dressing of honey and cream, and . . . watercress and almonds in a goatsmilk yogurt. Whoopee!

EXOTIC FRUITS

Exotic fruits are now on the market. While initially they seem expensive, they are by far the one extravagance that you should allow yourself. They tend to get cheaper if you buy them in any quantity, and often appear on the wholesale lists but are passed by by your local greengrocer for lack of his knowing that you have hidden yearnings! Have a chat with him or her and talk with your friends. Among a group of my friends I found enough orders to keep us all supplied with persimmons (kaki fruit) for the entire December season. In our illustration, we show not only the round orange persimmons (which must be allowed to ripen unless you want the ultimate pucker—they are ripe when the pulp gets translucent and jelly-like under the skin), but also the Chinese gooseberry (or Kiwi fruit) which has a delightful green pulp reminiscent of strawberries and pineapple under its fuzzy exterior, the melons (smell the stem end, and don't buy unless you get melon fragrance—unless you care to wait awhile), the paw paws (or papaya), and the mangos are tropical, and will require some expert advice from your fruiterer. Wild berries you should go out and pick, but don't eat some unknown berry until you ask about it. Even the infallible test of eating only what the birds eat can be true only for the birds.

The bottom fruit is a pomegranate (pommey-grenade Seth says!) full of vitamin C.

Cumquats

One of the most robust of exotic fruits is the cumquat—introduced from China where, with its cousin the loquat, it has long graced the supper table as a preserve to eat with baked rice dishes, and as a sweet. The season is short, unless you have access to a Chinese grocery store, so when this piquant fruit appears in its small boxes, buy plenty. If you've never seen one, imagine a plum-sized orange with a flavour of lime and pineapple. They have the virtue of being completely and easily preserved as follows:

1lb (500g) of fresh cumquats can be simmered in 1pt (570ml, $2\frac{1}{2}$ cups) of water with sufficient brown sugar or honey to sweeten. Add at least 1 tsp of ginger, preferably freshly grated. (Note: it's best to prick tiny holes in each cumquat with a fork so that the juices inside easily merge with the syrup.) When done (about 20 min) the fruits will have turned translucent and the syrup will be quite thick. One friend has cooked with blackstrap molasses—the result was memorable, if a little indelicate!

Cursio's Salad for Health

This is a salad bowl that is a meal in itself, especially in the summer when the ingredients are plentiful.

Toss together:

1 head of small lettuce, well washed, dried and patted out on a tea towel
2 medium garden tomatoes
½ unwaxed cucumber
4-5 stalks of celery (optional)
several torn apart stems of parsley

Coat with 4 tbsp olive or sesame oil mixed with 4 tbsp Brewer's yeast and dash of vegetable salt. Use the pepper grinder if you wish. Cottage cheese, spring onions, green peppers and croutons are all optional ingredients. Eat immediately, *not* out of the refrigerator.

Green Pepper Salad

Sometime in the summer or early autumn, green peppers (and their flashy yellow and red cousins) suddenly take a dramatic turn towards cheapness in the market. They cease to be waxed, and seem to acquire a new pungency. Slice 1 pepper (that Peter picked for pretty Priscilla!) per person and cut into as thin a set of slices as your best stainless steel knife will do, and still leave you with the fingers with which to eat. Add a few plum tomatoes, and serve in an olive oil vinaigrette with a few capers. Dash with paprika. Eat with pumpernickle or black bread. Relax and follow with a cup of camomile tea. Congratulate yourself for eating healthily, savouring the last tastes.

Astrid's Tomato and Ginger

You've just acquired lots of plump tomatoes, perhaps by going out and picking them or struggling with crowds at the open market. Shopping day fatigue and feeling jaded with heat? The restorative is as below:

Cut up at least 3 medium to large tomatoes per person, deseeding if you wish. Next pull apart several large stems of parsley, cut up a spring onion or two, and perhaps some rings of green pepper. Grate fresh ginger into 4 fl oz (115ml, ½ cup) sour cream or yogurt. Put all into a wooden salad bowl and stir about until the cream is pinked with the tomato juice. Breath-taking.

Courgette (Zucchini) Salad

A previously unknown salad ingredient is now more often to be found in the markets—small to medium courgettes. Best when very young.

Grate together courgettes (1 or 2 per serving) with same number of young carrots. Sprinkle sparingly with sea salt and dill. Coat with a vinaigrette dressing and grind on a bit of peppercorn. Garnish with small gherkins, radish roses, or black olives. Such a nice change from cucumbers.

Red (Purple) Cabbage

A cut open purple cabbage has such a beautiful colouring that it can be simply gazed upon— but the gazing may be a bit indiscreet unless the cabbage has a proper dressing! May I suggest that:

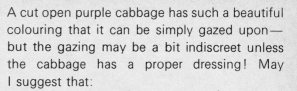

2-3 tbsp green olive oil
2-3 tbsp yogurt or full milk
2 tbsp honey
1 tsp dried mustard
2 tsp lime juice (fresh or Roses)
1 squeeze garlic press
2 dashes vegetable salt

be put in a cup, whisked, and poured fresh on the shredded cabbage.

Simple Cabbage Salad

Grated cabbage can be combined with bananas, cut apples and walnuts, and topped with a yogurt dressing made with lemon juice, honey and a dash of Ribena. Bean sprouts mixed with grated carrots, raw peanuts, a little cream and lemon juice—cardamom powder, and much munch and crunch.

Fennel Salad

This wild or cultivated herb makes the nicest of salads for the Italian pasta dishes (pp 59-62). In combination with dandelion greens it is absolutely mind-expanding. And if your friends are dining with you, one of the few times when a garlic dressing is not completely anti-social . . .

VEGETABLES

CABBAGES

Cabbage is continued here to introduce the vegetable section of this book as its cheapness and versatility are surpassed only by its elegance. The advice we give now about cabbages is true of all green leafys: don't over-cook; don't boil; do remember to make infusions of herbs in the cooking water.

Stellar Cabbage

A simple recipe first:

Cut a cabbage into 6-8 wedges starting from the top and leaving the stem in as a holder. Or cut a small cabbage into stars as in the illustration. Place in a large, comfortable pan where you have simmered herbs such as chervil or tarragon in 4 fl oz (115ml, ½ cup) water. Allow the water to heat to the steaming point, and turn off the heat. Make sure the lid is tight and leave. In 5 min or so, if the cabbage has turned to a bright green (or deep purple in the case of the red cabbage), remove it at once. It's now ready to eat.

Now, the fun begins. Grate a soft English cheese over the top. Make up and pour on a yogurt and dill dressing (p91). Arrange slices of pimento (see p90) as rays to the star. Serve with our tomato ginger salad (p29). A meal in itself.

Cabbage Packets

Take the large outer leaves of a cabbage and steam in a basket over boiling water for just a few minutes to make them pliable. Cook a stuffing of:

4oz (125g, 1 cup) buckwheat groats (protein)
1oz (30g, ¼ cup) ground nuts or chestnuts
1oz (30g, ¼ cup) soy grits, or meat substitute
1oz (30g, ¼ cup) seeded raisins or currants (iron)
3 tbsp (or less) Brewer's yeast (for B-complex)
1 or 2 tbsp fresh parsley (for carotene)
2 fl oz (60ml, ¼ cup) water with soysauce or 2 tbsp Marmite (for the rest)

Place a portion of stuffing in the centre of each leaf (the above makes 6 portions), roll up and secure with kebab skewer, or tie with white thread. Shred the cabbage inside the stuffing leaves, and line a buttered casserole dish. Arrange the stuffed ones on top. Cover and bake for almost 20 min at 300°F, 150°C, mark 1-2, adding water if needed, to keep moist.
Another stuffing:

6oz (180g, 1½ cups) rice, hopefully brown, cooked
2 sliced green peppers (especially those turning red)
4oz (125g) mushrooms cooked in margarine
and sage
cream to moisten, or cream cheese

Other wrappers:
15-20 parboiled grape leaves or large collard leaves. Add bits of nuts, onions, tomato, pine-apple. Who hates cabbage? Not your guests.

THE 'OTHER' CABBAGES

We used the heading cabbages in the plural. There is a reason botanically speaking for this, as broccoli, Brussel sprouts and cauliflowers are all developed parts of that same plant, the cabbage. They all suffer from over-cooking, and are invariably smothered in a white pasty goo. On to the remedy. Never more than a minute or so in a little bubbly, boiling water, then off with the heat, and up with the vitamin retention curve. Save the waters for any sauce, or keep for a soup (see p15). Try:

broccoli spears, cut lengthwise, treated as delicately as asparagas, in a butter sauce full of chopped almonds;

cauliflower fronds coated in milk and rice flour and deep fried for 30 sec, Japanese tempura style (p68);

Brussels sprouts treated as rare fruits, split in the middle and stuffed with cream cheese and capers;

broccoli in a paprika sauce made of Camembert melted with 3 tsp paprika (the real Hungarian kind);

cauliflower in a green sauce of melted cream cheese coloured with chopped chives, torn apart parsley, spring onions, and pulled apart spinach;

or cauliflower fronds matched weight for weight with large cubes of fresh pear and cavorting in a cream, wholewheat flour and curry sauce. Oh Yes! The Cabbages.

GREENS

Eat all those vitamin rich tops of mustard, beets, turnips, collards, kale, Swiss chard, kohlrabi, and even some wild ones. But greens are only as delicate in flavour as you are in cooking. So cook sparingly, only until they turn a deeper shade of green, and be prepared to chew— which is good for you anyway. Savour the flavour; choose herbs carefully, and eat plate- fuls with brown rice or fresh carrot juice. French goat cheeses (chevres) are the best marriages. Don't forget dandelion leaves (p88).

Cauliflower Croquettes

Crisp cauliflower fronds in ice cold water. Dip in milk, or better yet sour cream, and then roll in flour (unbleached white, or a darker one if you like). Or shake in a bag of flour and onion bits. You may need to dip a few times to get a thick coating. Sprinkle with coriander, and drop into a skillet full of melted margarine. Fry until golden brown. A Norwegian artist first made this while her guests looked out over the deep blue fjords.

Rotegrot (p82) is the perfect dessert, mu tea (p94) delightful after that, and then a long walk. Flowers. Cauliflowers. See Cauliflower Soup Chantilly (p16).

Belgian Endive (Chicory)

The royal green leafy is, without a doubt, Belgian endive. Expensive most of the year, it has a short season in the late Spring of being reasonable. When small, the heads can be cooked whole, or if a bit larger the endive can be cut into halves or quarters. Bitter of taste, it calls for a delicate sauce.

A French friend always cuts endives in half and cooks them in a frying pan with the slightest bit of butter, cut side down. When the butter begins to sizzle, she adds a few tbsp of hot water and then covers the pan. When steam forms (30-45 sec) she removes the lid. The endive will begin to open, and spread its leaves like a peacock. Cook a minute or two more, remove the endive from the pan, and put in a warm, covered bowl—it must be pampered.

CHEESE SAUCE

Sprinkle 1oz (30g, ¼ cup) flour onto the remaining butter and fry for a few seconds. Pour in 4 fl oz (115ml, ½ cup) of milk slowly, stirring all the while. When bubbling, add grated dry cheese—Swiss, Schabzier (rennet free) is perfect—and blend.

Grate a few Brazil nuts over the sauce and pour on the endive. Serve. Great with string quartets, or trumpet fanfares. Baroque.

SPINACH

If endive is royalty, spinach is pure democracy. Plentiful most of the year, its glory is to be in the spinach pasta on p 61. But it can, and should, be eaten solo as often as it is on the market. When young and tender, the fresh leaves are superb as a salad, especially with a sourcream dressing with a dash of dried mustard, a few sesame seeds, and a few celery leaves. When slightly older, cook the leaves for just minutes in 2 fl oz (60ml, ¼ cup) or less water with a dash of fresh lime, or vinegar, and pinches of mace. Eat all alone.

Spinach Pie

Then, should you be in one of the big cities, you may find yourself with some Greek Feta cheese which you can fry and cube into the spinach, or if your luck really is good, you may purchase a packet of filo pastry leaves and make a spinach pie (spanikotiropeta). But filo or not, a simple pastry (see p 51) makes the delicacy possible. Roll the pastry as thin as possible, and cut into squares. Cut a diagonal across, and you have triangles. Or fold. In either case use one triangle as the base and put on a lump of Feta and a spoonful of cooked spinach. Top with another triangle, and crimp the edges shut. Brush with butter and bake in a 400°F, 205°C, mark 6 oven on an oiled baking sheet for about 10 min until brown and puffed.

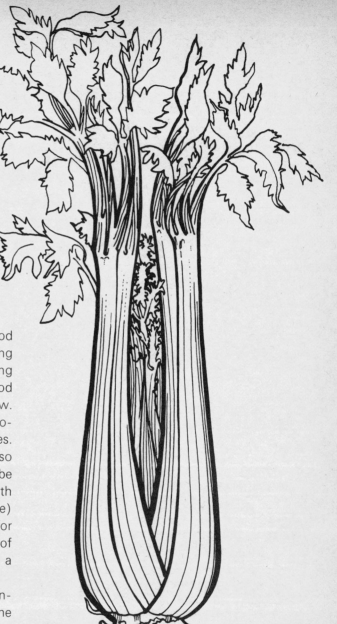

CELERY

Celery stalks, sold usually covered in good English dirt to keep fresh, I'm told, are beginning to appear with some regularity without being more than 10 per cent spoiled! They do a good job of adding natural salts to any soup or stew. Celery seed and leafy tops are always appropriate additions to casseroles and pasta dishes. Chopped in 1 in long fingers they can be ever so slightly cooked but should never, never be boiled. Braising for 2 min in butter, with croutons, tops as well (and a dash of sage) makes a calorieless casserole (about 60 for the whole celery). This dish invites the use of chervil, that delicate parsley-like herb, or a mere touch of anise.

Chinese cabbage, seen in the best greengrocers only, is a delightful replacement in the above recipes.

Celeriac in Orange Sauce

The root of the celery plant, as the root of the parsley is, in some varieties, likely to grow quite large. It is edible and is often sold under the name of celeriac. Choose medium sized ones, and be prepared to do a good washing and scrubbing. Parboil in a water infused with caraway seeds or a bouquet garni, for 20 min or more, until the root is soft when a fork is inserted. Make up a sauce of 3oz (85g, ½ cup) brown flour stirred into a small can of tomato paste, whipped until smooth. Thin with the juice and pulp of 2-3 oranges. Put on the grill and cut the celeriac into thick slices. Pour sauce over and grill for 5 min until the sauce is absorbed. Be sure to use an ovenproof dish. Serve garnished with a Bel Paese or Beaumont cheese and a bit of grated orange peel.

Hot Cucumbers

Cucumbers can be cooked, as well as being in salads. Cut thin slices and put in a pan with very little water. Dill is the usual spice, but tumeric or summer savoury are also enhancing. Serve with yogurt liberally sprinkled with paprika.

Russians and Poles are fond of cold cucumbers covered with honey. The South Indians make raita by mixing yogurt and chopped cucumber, onion, peppers, and bits of mango.

Radishes

Real peasant food. Serve with the mamaliga on p 50. You may have had radish tops as a green, but the whole plant can be cooked, especially the black radish that is beginning to show up from the continent. Slice 3 or 4 small bunches of radishes fairly thin and tear apart the tops. Boil up 1qt (1l) of infused water (coriander is good), and cook the radishes for 7-10 min. Meanwhile, tear apart one bunch of parsley. When the radishes are done, drain them and add to parsley in a frying pan with sufficient butter, then fry for just a few minutes. A Yugoslavian delicacy, and a tonic as well.

Pungent Tomatoes

2 large sweet onions
6 large, perfectly ripe tomatoes
oil for frying
curry powder to taste
Major Grey's Mango Chutney as desired
4 toasted slices of homemade whole wheat bread
salt and pepper

Brown the peeled, sliced onions in the oil, then place them in the bottom of a greased casserole. Add a layer of thick tomato slices and sprinkle with salt, freshly ground black pepper, and the curry powder. Bake in a medium hot oven, 350°F, 180°C, mark 4, for 10 min. While the tomatoes are baking, spread the chutney on the bread, and arrange the bread slices on a serving dish. Pile the tomatoes and onions on the bread slices, and serve.

Haricots Verts

The summer is buzzing with bees making honey, the hot days are almost over, and the long green bean appears on the market. Snap off the ends while infusing a little water with basil, drop the beans in, take out in 4-5 min. Butter. That's it, folks. By the plateful.

Note: Leftover beans can be mixed with freshly fried mushrooms, almonds, and a whole wheat cream sauce for a great casserole. Tarragon is recommended as the spice, and a small dash of paprika.

Ratatouille

Here are some hints for making this French dish in a delicious, non-greasy form:

Use only small to medium aubergines that are firm and free of soft spots. Try to obtain the real green olive oil from the first pressings. Avoid bloated greenhouse tomatoes. The garlic should enhance the flavour, not drown it.

The method is simple. Fry 2 large seeded green peppers with 2 medium onions in sufficient olive oil to keep from burning (not so much as create swimming conditions!) This should take about 5 min. Meanwhile cut up ½lb (250g) tomatoes into wedges, deseeding if you wish. Put aside. Cut up 2 small-to-medium aubergines (egg plants) into small slices (making circles) about ¼ in thick (about ½cm) and, if possible, fry in a separate pan in very little olive oil until slightly browned and yet soft in the centre. (Some salt the slices, then rinse to remove bitterness.) Add aubergine to the peppers and onions, cook a minute then add tomatoes. Turn off heat, cover with a lid, and in one minute remove. Serve with pepper grinder at the table and bowls of parmesan cheese. Decorate with a bit of cress if you wish.

Thinly-sliced aubergines can be dipped into milk, coated with crumbs and flour and fried in olive oil. Serve sprinkled with cheese and a bit of lemon juice.

Beet Tops

If you have to serve a crowd, or are cooking for a family, a rich-in-minerals dish can be made from the beetroot leaves that normally get left behind.

2 bunches of young beetroot leaves
finely chopped yellow or red onions
2 tbsp safflower oil
1 vegetable bouillon cube
½ tsp finely cut garlic
1 bay leaf
1 tsp sweet paprika
chopped green pepper
diced celery
2 tbsp whole wheat flour
4 fl oz (115ml, ½ cup) water
fingers of toasted whole wheat bread

Tear the leaves into small pieces and parboil in boiling water for only 1 min. Remove and drain. Brown the onions in oil and then crush the bouillon cube over them. Add beet leaves, pepper, celery, and herbs. Simmer for 10 min. Make a paste of the flour and water (use the water from cooking the leaves), and stir in. Thicken for 2-3 min, stirring well. Ready for serving on fingers of whole wheat toast.

Serve with the Tomato and Ginger salad on p29.

Stuffed Courgettes (Zucchini)

As the illustration shows, the courgette is stuffed by forcing a hole through its entirety with a small metal or wooden rod (don't use your husband's or wife's electric drill). They can also be stuffed by cutting a wedge out of the top of one side. The object in either case is not only to create a cavity for the the stuffing, but to remove the seeds.

One simple stuffing is to cube a number of slices of dried or whole wheat bread and fry in margarine with a good number of dashes of sage, adding just enough milk to make mushy.

A more elegant stuffing, and the one that is shown, is made by cutting up a cauliflower into individual fronds. Steam for just a minute, pour over a cheese sauce (see p33) and then put into the courgette with a funnel. An obvious piece of advice is to be sure to close one end while stuffing. Place the courgettes in a moderate oven (350°F, 180°C, mark 4) for about 35-45 min. A vegetable marrow may be used for this recipe when in season, but will need more baking if large.

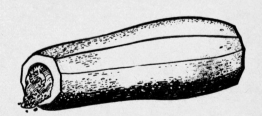

ASPARAGUS

The asparagus is not only an aesthetic delight but a culinary one as well. An acceptable vegetable when frozen, it must not be thawed out in advance of cooking. But fresh, whether green or white, it must be cooked only for minutes so as not to remove the crispness. Trim the purple white ends off to within a small finger's width from the green. Rinse carefully to remove any sand lurking in the tips as well as in the leaf-like structures on the stem. Cook either standing up tied in a bunch, in just enough water to steam; or lay out one deep in a large skillet, with just enough water to cover the bottom of the pan. In either case the cooking time is just 5 min, and the result will be deep green and a little chewy—in short, the taste of spring. You may wish to infuse the cooking water with basil, thyme, or add the traditional bay leaf and lavender to give the Provençal touch. Garnishes should remain simple, unless as I do, you eat asparagus almost every day of the season. In which case, butter sauces made with the cooking liquids, and various of the mustards (such as the aged Dijons) add just that bit of piquancy. Or nasturtium buds (capers) in fresh cream. Or horrify your French friends and cut slices of Brie to lay over, and melt into hot asparagus. Mais, monsieur et madame, c'est delicieux, pourquoi pas?

SOYBEAN SPROUTS

If you simply put soybeans in water, as some have tried, they just rot. The answer as in all farming is good drainage—in this case, any netting cloth over a bowl, or an old pot with holes punched in the bottom. Soak the beans (mung, white, pink, you name it) overnight, or for a day, and then pile on top of the drainer. Sprinkle on warm water three or four times a day, being sure that the water drains off. After four or more days the sprouts will have appeared, and you can harvest, keeping the sprouts in the vegetable part of the fridge.

LADIES FINGERS (OKRA)

This green vegetable is known more to the warmer part of the world than in Northern Europe, and can become a delicacy if handled carefully. You will most frequently encounter it in Indian restuarants where it will either be hidden in a curry, or fried in a dough as a bhajee. It is found as well in the course of a short Middle Eastern season, and in frozen packets. Dipped in milk, rolled in a light flour and maize meal mixture, and then gently fried in sesame or safflower oil, it is great fun for genuine licking of the fingers. Stewed carefully for just minutes, the okra will turn bright green. Drain, add butter and squeeze a lemon a few times to reduce sliminess. If you do find them in a shop, be sure they are small to medium ones as those which are large are also woody and bitterly pithy.

LEEKS

No more limp leeks! Sweet and crisp—not soggy 'smush'. After washing thoroughly—look for the dirt and sand in crevices, cut the leeks into 1 in (2·5cm) slices. Heat several slices of butter in a pan and put in the leeks. When the butter commences sizzling, drop in 2-3 tbsp warm water. Cover and let steam for a few min only. The leeks are done when the leaves are deep green and have loosened. (Steam-frying is a good technique for other vegetables as well.) Remove leeks from heat and put a few tbsp of a green boursin or a handful of grated Cheshire. Caerphilly if you will, but a Welsh epicure I know does refer to it as English soap! Nutmeg sprinkled over the whole is nice, or try a bit of grated burdock.

Leekburgers

Leeks (4-5 medium large) can also be finely chopped with 1 medium onion. Cook in just a little water, then mix with 2oz (60g, $\frac{1}{2}$ cup) whole wheat bread crumbs and 4 tbsp milk. Add dashes of sage and mould in a burger shape. Fry with enough vegetable oil to prevent sticking. Nuts, carrots (grated) and bits of beetroot will vary what should become an easy favourite. Serve solo or in a sandwich made with whole wheat bread.

CARROTS

Crisp carroty crunch. This is the sound of health as is the munch of celery or the crack of an old-fashioned eating apple (such as the almost vanished 'black stem' variety). They certainly aren't anti-social sounds, so have a jam session, for these crisps are good for the digestion, contain rejuvenating vitamins, and have a minimum of calories. Perfect in the pantry for warding off snack inches. Carrots lightly cooked are a weekly menu idea. They can provide an opportunity for herbal education as well. Cook them in infusions made of basil, tarragon, coriander, mace, savoury, mint, a pressing of garlic, rosemary, or homemade curry. Create dramatic mixes, or create magic by the addition of extras in the liquid such as sultanas with the curry, or artichoke roots with the mace, and so on. Add sauces, if not too often. Or capers if you like them. Don't spoil all this effort by overcooking, carrots only need a few minutes. And simply give a good brushing, there is no need to scrape the vitamins off. Nut loafs made with carrots (p 83) and carrot cake (p 76) complete the picture.

PARSNIPS

Parsnips suffer a lot, often ending up as dry dreary sticks with the only virtue of being inconspicuous in the roasted dinner. Rethinking allows them to become a texture for stews, an addition to other roots, or the main attraction itself. Cut lengthwise into quarters and sautée in a few tbsp of butter. If softening is wanted add a few tbsp of soy sauce, or a vegex cube dissolved in water, and create a bit of steam under the lid. Garnish with winter savoury.

Or slice into moons and cook with half a dozen sliced mushrooms, a bit of grated carrot, and pieces of gluten (p 56) for just minutes.

Serve with purple cabbage salad (p 29) or cranberry salad (p 23).

If you feel adventurous, get some Tekka powder from a shop that stocks macrobiotic supplies, and fry parsnips in a mixture of Tekka and aged soybean sauce. Try once or twice a year to preserve the astonishment your mouth will receive—especially if garnished with a little Japanese spiced horseradish!

ARTICHOKES

Globe Artichokes

There are, as the drawing shows, two types of artichokes, the globe which is the green fruit of a thistle relative and the Jerusalem which is the root of a sunflower relative. Globe artichokes are a bother to eat but, if you wish to slow down your eating and have all the fun of opening Christmas presents, they will repay you with their delightful taste. They are best cooked in a large pot, that will accommodate 4 or more at a time. Be sure to rinse them out thoroughly in case they contain sand. Make an infusion of thyme and mustard in a pot full of water, and boil for a few moments before adding the artichokes. About 15-25 min of cooking is sufficient, but the only real way to know that they are ready involves pulling a leaf from the centre. When it comes out easily, bite the end to check for flavour and softness. You should be able to scrape it off between your teeth. Lift the artichoke you are testing with a large spoon or a pair of tongs unless you are both quick-fingered and witted. Drain when done, and eat leaf by leaf until the choke of fuzzy thistles is reached. Cut it out, and enjoy the bottom or 'heart'. Extra and traditional pleasure is had by making a sauce for dipping the leaves in. Mix cream with a dash of mustard, dill and coriander; or melt a French banon cheese; or heat a vinaigrette dressing with grated parmesan; or press garlic cloves into yogurt.

Jerusalem Artichokes

While a staple ingredient in stews and with parsnips (with capers), these roots are a true delicacy when sliced across their length and fried in olive oil with a bit of sage as a complement. Serve solo or under a bit of melted cheese. Can also be shredded and cooked with a bit of butter and soy sauce. Serve with horseradish, or prepared Dijon mustard. The small French variety, 'stracheys', are the best of all!

AVOCADOS

The avocado is unique among fruits for being full of rich oils and, when soft and creamy, unique for its perfect edibility. Put in paper bags to ripen perfectly. We have already given you the means to make it into a soup (Sopa del Aguacate p18), and will now discuss it as a salad (guacamole) and as a dessert.

Guacamole

The best guacamoles all seem to have one special spice in common, cumin seeds, or cominos as they are known in Spanish, nicely ground up. The spice is worth searching for, and happily is included in any number of the 'sets' in supermarkets as well as in packets in Indian and speciality shops. For each two servings, cut the avocado as shown here (why shouldn't you give you and yours a party setting?) or just into two parts. Scoop out the pulp after removing the seed (which has its uses as well in growing a lovely green plant). Mash gently with a fork or spoon, and add $\frac{1}{2}$ tsp cumin per serving, a dash of chili pepper if you like, 1 tbsp lemon or lime juice, $\frac{1}{4}$ of an onion chopped, a little olive oil (or avocado oil), and a diced medium tomato. Mix together, and spoon back into the shell as shown. Slip freshly cooked asparagus tips in for complete elegance.

Avocado Sweet

Avocado as a fruit is what we aim to discuss now, ma'm or sir, and we know that you will have to overcome some certain prejudices. But a wise Brazilian not only told us about this, but made it. What is most difficult is the second ingredient—an eggless ice-cream. But ask about, and some local dairy may be selling a soy-based iced dessert that will be just right. Or get some double cream. In either case, whip up the avocado into a foamy froth, add the ice-cream or cream, a spoonful of instant coffee, or several grinds of nutmeg, sprinkle on cardamom, one squeeze of a lime, and beat some more. Put into an emptied ice-cube tray in the ice compartment. Serve scooped into balls, topped with fresh mint leaves, either in the avocado shells, or on biscuits. Magnifico.

To grow the avocado, keep it suspended in water, in a large glass, with tooth picks pressed into the sides, as shown. Change the water constantly to keep rot away, and keep in a warm setting, even in a greenhouse. When the tap root is well established, pot in a good soil. The seed may very well stay with the plant above the potting soil. You'll need years, and differently sexed plants to ever be growing your own. Who knows . . . ?

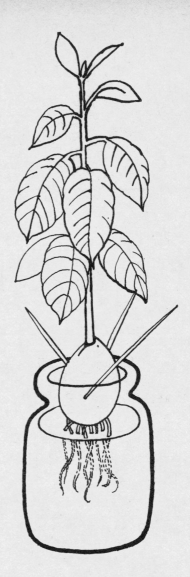

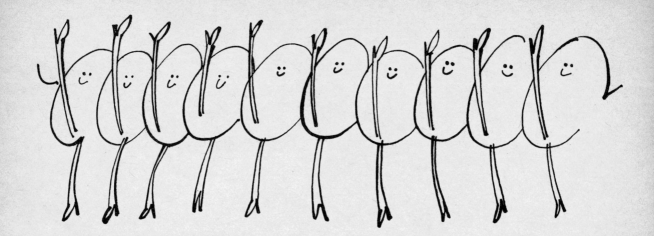

POTATOES

The disrepute of potatoes probably dates back to the 19th-century famines in Ireland. But this South American plant, like its cousin the tomato, which once suffered the stigma of being thought of as the apple from Eden, deserves a good reputation. This is especially true in England where the potato gives up to one third of the vitamin C of the winter diet. The newer the potato, the type of cooking (baking is best), and the amount of peel left on (hopefully all) can enhance the amount of vitamins, especially ascorbic acid, by as much as three or four times. Mashing, for instance, halves the mineral content and often destroys the vitamins. Potatophobia about calories is stranger still, as the potato is 80 per cent water and only 24 calories per oz (crisps are 159).

Baked Cheesey Potato

One recipe with which to learn about liking potatoes in their skins is to bake first, then slice and add to a pan of fried green peppers and chives. Top with soft cheese and enjoy with a simple cabbage salad (p 29). Or take the above, add 4 fl oz (115ml, ½ cup) milk, and bake for 20 min in a moderate (350°F, 180°C, mark 4) oven. Wonderful on winter nights.

44

Potato Flan

This is the perfect recipe for enhancing the taste of the mashed potato, and is just the thing to serve to some of your non-veggie friends who think that a pile of mash is just the thing to serve you. Simple, yet quite sophisticated in its own way.

With the mash potato from 3-4 medium-sized, not too old potatoes (with the skins if you like) make a mixture with 2oz (60g, ½ cup) whole wheat or rye flour and 2oz (60g, 4 tbsp) butter. The mixture must be thick. Let it cool, and then press into an 8in (15cm) flan tin and shape, building up the sides to make a 'crust'.

Put oven on at 400°F (200°C, mark 6). In a saucepan, fry 2 or 3 medium onions with 12 small mushrooms until brown. Remove and set aside mushrooms. Add 1oz (30g, ¼ cup) whole wheat flour gradually and make a roux. Then stir in ½pt (285ml, 1¼ cups) whole milk. Cook sauce until thick. Whip in 4oz (125g) medium hard cheese with generous dashes of coriander or mace, and several stalks of parsley or spring onions. Pour into the potato 'pastry' and decorate the top with a circle of mushrooms. Bake for 25 min in centre of oven.

Nicest with fresh asparagus or serve with a tossed green salad, such as Cursio's on p28. Can also be decorated with small plum tomatoes.

Baked Sweet Potatoes

These potatoes (and not the root known as yams) are a marvellous addition to any table. The small to medium ones are grand cooked in the following manner:

1 or 2 well-washed potatoes per person
1 tsp powdered cloves
¼ tsp allspice
½ tsp cinnamon
butter or sesame oil

Wrap each sweet potato in a foil packet so that a small box is formed around each potato. Put in the spices and add two pats of butter. Seal and bake for about 30 min in a medium hot oven, 375°F (190°C, mark 5), or until you are sure they are done. Grand.

Baked Stuffed Potatoes

These recipes call for one medium-to-large potato per serving, and come with as many variations as there are cheeses and 'extra' ingredients. It's perfectly possible to eat a potato twice a week, 52 weeks a year, and *never* repeat the taste or even the texture! Not that the *Guinness Book of Records* has any entry to be broken. Unless you happen to like baking the potato in a lump of mud on an open fire (which is to be recommended), 'fings' has improved since this root was discovered. Wash carefully, removing spots. Oil the skin to make soft and to seal in vitamins. Wrap in foil to speed cooking and bake at 375°F (190°C, mark 5). Plain Jane potatoes—butter and parsley, sour cream and chives—are good enough. Or:

Cheddar Potatoes

Cut the potato in half after baking, and use fingers to 'break-up' the insides. Cover with cheddar, a dash of paprika, and bit of tarragon rubbed between the fingers, tiny bits of onion, and a grind of black pepper. Pop back into the oven or under the grill until cheese is bubbly.

Surprise Potatoes

Examine the fridge, and come up with mashed chick peas, bits of pineapple, a few pine nuts and a little raunchy Liderkranz. Add to cooked potato. Or . . .

Potato Marron

Remove the 'meat' from the potato after it has cooled awhile, and mash with a lump of margarine or butter. Add 1 tbsp of mashed chestnut or marron paste to taste, and 8 or 9 chopped nuts, such as walnuts. Add tiny pieces of chive and diced green pepper (not much) and put all the mash into a pastry bag. Force out into the potato shells and form roses or sun flowers. Dash on some paprika and crumbles of Brie for a glaze, and put under a grill for time enough to brown the tops. See the illustration below.

WHOLE GRAINS

The *whole* truth is that the extraction of the outside of grains is a crime, especially in these days of refrigeration. A friend who owns a fine natural foods store simply keeps her flours chilled all summer and never has had spoilage. So why do 'they' do it? Because we keep buying. If we stop, so will they.

An example of what I'm talking about is brown rice which has eight times the thiamine (B_1), five times the nicotinic acid (Niacin), and three times the B_2 of boiled white rice. The same type of figures are true for whole wheat breads and white, brown sugars and white. It takes more than dried milk powder and chemicals to restore the value. So here we give you some help, along with the hope that you will try rye, bulk wheat and barley flours, as well as eating the grains soaked in water overnight and steamed—such as kasha, couscous, groats, and oat meals for supper.

Kasha

Sort over fresh buckwheat, removing any black grains. Roast 1lb (500g) in a heavy ungreased frying pan until it goes pale yellow. Add 1 tsp sea salt, and 2oz (60g, 4 tbsp) butter and enough boiling water to cover. Stew for about 30 min, or until soft. Serve with beet croquettes (p19). Spice with celery or burdock.

BREAKFAST GRAINS

OATMEALS

Oatmeal is the normal diet, so we are told, of those who live North of Hadrian's Wall. It becomes a marvellous breakfast grain, if it is cooked with the addition of pieces of apple, pears, fresh peaches, plums, dried pears, apricots or peaches in the winter, nuts, coconuts, fresh-picked or dew-dropped berries, or any of the various fruits that attract or appeal to you. The basic recipe calls for:

1pt (570ml, 2½ cups) water
4oz (125g, 1 cup) oatmeal
2oz (60g, ½ cup) coconut
2oz (60g, ½ cup) chopped nuts and raisins
and, for your health, 1oz (30g, ¼ cup) Brewers' yeast
or natural wheat germ

Add a dash of sea salt, and brown sugar and honey to taste if you desire. Bring the water to boil, then stir in all the ingredients except the oatmeal. Cook for several minutes, and when the mixture begins to bubble again, add the oatmeal. Cook on a lower heat for about 5 min more until the mixture is of sufficient thickness. Serve with milk or fresh cream.

Muesli

Muesli has begun to be available commercially, and unfortunately it is also available in adulterated forms. Beware of products that have dried skimmed milk powder, white sugar or an alphabet of preservatives. Make your own as follows:

4 tbsp rolled oats
2 tbsp fresh lemon juice
4oz (125g, 1 cup) chopped walnuts, almonds
or cashews
2 sliced bananas
1 or 2 large unsprayed chopped apples
raw sugar or honey if you like
1 carton (5oz, 150g) of plain whole milk yogurt

Simply mix the ingredients together and serve. If you wish to save time, the dried ingredients can be premixed and stored, and you simply add each day the fruit or nut that appeals to you.

Cream of Wheat (Semolina)

Start with an infusion of water with milk, and such dried fruit as you like (or fresh fruit, such as pears or apples), you need add only 3 tbsp of semolina per 8 fl oz (228ml, 1 cup) of liquid. Blend in slowly to avoid lumps, or mix semolina with cold water, and stir into the hot mixture. When bubbly, remove from heat, and add either dried yeast or wheat germ for additional nutrition, or the daily supply of nuts. Fresh cherries (pitted) and almonds are grand this way.

RICE

We have already told you of the food values to be gained by eating brown rice rather than white, and you will find rice to be a good protein if you consult p 63. To prepare for 4-6 servings: Cook 1lb (500g, 2 cups) brown rice in $1\frac{1}{2}$ pints (855ml, $3\frac{1}{2}$ cups) water—preferably a water infused with the herbs and spices appropriate to its end use (cinnamon for breakfast, cardamom for dessert, basil for a vegetable). After bringing to a boil, turn heat down, and after 30 min (plus) the water should all be absorbed. Serve as is with a butter sauce into which you have heated leaves of mint, green spring onions, a green pepper and a bit of pimento.

Rice Cakes

The illustration opposite gives some idea of the shape and consistency of the rice cake. What is missing of course is the taste and flavour. But these you can have for doing the following. Cook brown rice as per instructions or use leftovers. Stir in brown flour at a ratio of one portion flour for each two portions of rice. Add chopped onions, green pepper, parsley, sufficient milk to make a dough. Shape into patties and fry in $\frac{1}{2}$in (1cm) vegetable oil until one side is done. Turn with a spatula and cook the other side until light brown. Herbs and spices as you please.

Rice Fritters

Make up the flour/rice mixture, using yogurt to make moist. Add cut up fresh pears, or apple, or pineapple or plums (or use all) and fry as above. Angelica or cardamom are just the spices.

Mamaliga

This Rumanian delicacy has a peasant background. It is quite related to the Italian polenta. Its basic ingredient, a meal made from maize, you will find called either polenta or corn meal. For each 2 servings you need:

½pt (285ml, 1¼ cups) salted boiling wàter
5oz (150g, 1¼ cups) yellow corn meal
1 bunch small spring onions or scallions cut
into pieces
4oz (125g, 1 cup) cubed Cheddar or French
Beaumont cheese (or the real one, kaimar, p72)

Slowly stir the corn meal into the salted water, adding a few leaves of thyme. After cooking over a medium heat for 10 min, or until quite thick, add the onions and cook for 2-3 min more. Remove from heat, and stir in the cheese and paprika. Serve in hot bowls, or let it chill and fry in squares, with soy sauce. For protein balance, make up a kidney bean salad.

Kidney Bean Salad

Drain 1 small can kidney beans, saving some of the liquid. Mix the liquid (about 6-8 tbsp) with an equal amount of sour cream or yogurt, blending in ½ tsp mustard powder, a dash of cumin powder, a small chopped onion, and cubes of pickle. Pour over the beans and serve cold.

Corn on the Cob

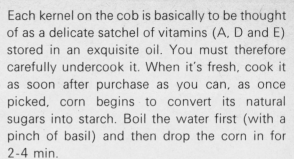

Each kernel on the cob is basically to be thought of as a delicate satchel of vitamins (A, D and E) stored in an exquisite oil. You must therefore carefully undercook it. When it's fresh, cook it as soon after purchase as you can, as once picked, corn begins to convert its natural sugars into starch. Boil the water first (with a pinch of basil) and then drop the corn in for 2-4 min.
(*Note:* the traditional test for freshness is to press one kernel, and if it spurts juice, well and good; if not, leave alone.)

Popcorn

In its pure state, popcorn bears no resemblance whatsoever to the stale confectionary found in certain cinemas. Moreover, it is salted and not sugared, and so is a low calorie treat. To make: heat a deep (3-4in) skillet, or a heavy saucepan (6-8in deep), and add just enough vegetable oil to coat the bottom thickly. Too little oil will cause burning and too much will fry the corn that has popped, causing it to stick. When a drop of water will splutter in the oil, add enough popcorn kernels to cover the bottom of the pan, put the lid on, and slowly shake the pan. After a minute or two, the corn will start popping, and will quickly fill the pan. Remove from the heat when the last grain pops, and turn into a large bowl. You can add brown sugar but sea salt is best.

PASTRY

All of the following recipes can be made by simply using flour, water and oil, and the simplest of these is pastry. If you are used to working with white flour you will find that the pastry from whole wheat flour is not only more tasty, but also more apt to crumble. This needn't be despaired over.

To make enough for a 9in pie tin. For each 4oz (125g, 1 cup) of pastry use 4oz (125g, 1 cup) whole wheat flour, 1 tsp of cold water, and 1 tbsp of oil. Mix together and roll out. You will find that the weather and the condition of the flour will change slightly the amount of flour that you need for an easily worked texture.

Tortillas

This is another oil, water, and flour creation, but with the addition of maize meal (known as corn meal in the States and polenta in much of Europe). It is traditionally an American Indian and Mexican dish, but has found its way to Spain. When fried, it resembles pancakes and can be eaten with syrups. Normally it is served with beans that have been mashed, and fried—often with bits of green pepper and onion. prepare as follows:

Mix 4-5 tbsp vegetable oil into 2oz (60g, ½ cup) maize meal and stir until oil throughly mixed. Then sift in 4oz (125g, 1 cup) whole wheat flour and ½ tsp sea salt. Knead until a firm, smooth texture is obtained. Let rest for 5 min and then knead again. Pinch off lumps the size of plums, and pat out into rounds between your palms. You should get 6-8 tortillas per batch. Let rest for a minute while heating a well-oiled pan. Fry for several minutes on a side, turning with a spatula. A topping of sour cream and avocado with parsley is stupendioso.

Scottish Flapjacks

Flapjack is one of those troublesome words, like chip, that means one thing in English English and another in American English, so the word will be given a Scottish meaning here and clarity will dawn upon us all. Which means simply that the word is used to describe a hearty version of the pancake elsewhere.

Oil a shallow tin with margarine. In a pan put 4oz (125g) of margarine and 4 level tbsp of golden syrup, or maple syrup or (if you like it) treacle. Leave until margarine is melted into the syrup. Remove from heat and mix in 3oz (90g, ⅔ cup) oatmeal (rolled oats), a grating or two of fresh nutmeg or a dash of allspice if you wish. Turn into the tin and bake in a moderate oven for 30-40 min (335°F, 170°C, mark 3). Remove from oven. Let cool for only 5 min before cutting, for otherwise flapjack will harden and cutting will crumble it. Keep in a closed 'cookie' jar.

Eggless Pancakes

A perfectly good pancake can be made without breaking the heart of a single chicken!

Sift 4oz (125g, 1 cup) whole wheat flour with a pinch of sea salt. Add 2-2½ tsp vegetable oil and ¼pt (140ml, ½ cup) milk (or sour milk). Blueberries, currants, sultanas, bits of peaches, apricots and so on may be added at this stage. Beat batter just enough to mix all the ingredients, but not too much. Fry with sufficient vegetable oil to cover the bottom. Add oil after each cake is finished, but make sure that it has time to get quite hot, as that is the secret. Use a spatula or flat knife to lift each cake over when one side is brown. The size and even the shape of the cakes can vary from small to large, from round to animal shapes and daisies, as you gain practice. Serve with more fresh fruit, or sprinkle with cinnamon and eat with honey. Or as you will. Cheeses and vegetables can be added, then the cake can be rolled.

Chinese Pancakes

Ah, the Celestial Pancake—used all over China, but particularly in the north.

1lb (500g, 3 cups) whole wheat flour
½ tsp sea salt
8 fl oz (230ml, 1 cup) boiling water
½ tbsp vegetable oil (sesame if you can)

The flour and salt should be sifted together several times, preferably with a fine flour sifter. This gives air and lightness to the pancake. Then the boiling water is mixed in with a spoon (or chopsticks if you care to be authentic). Keep stirring the dough, and when it is cool, knead lightly. Roll out on a floured board into a long sausage roll, thumb sized in diameter. Cut off 1 in long pieces (2·5cm) and flatten in the palm of your hand until round and thin. Brush with vegetable oil. Repeat until you have lots of rounds, and then pair them off. With a rolling pin, flatten the pairs out until they are about the size of small saucers. Fry in a lightly greased pan (skillet) until nicely brown on both sides. Continue until all the pancakes are made. It is a good idea to split them open as they are done and keep in a saucepan covered with a warm damp cloth. They are now ready to be stuffed.

Chipatis

This flatbread from India is most versatile. It is traditionally used to scoop up other foods when eating with the fingers, or eaten by itself as a snack. Make it by mixing one portion of whole wheat flour (100 per cent) to a half portion of water and a dash of salt—using 1 tsp of soy flour to help keep whole, or a bit of rye flour for flavour. 8oz flour (250g, 1½ cups) to 4 fl oz water (115ml, a scant ½ cup) will make approx 6 servings (or more, if you let the batter sit, and roll out quite thin).

STUFFINGS

You'll love stuffing chipatis or Chinese pancakes, and there are hundreds of ways to do them. At the table, spoon Bombay potatoes (p 66) on the centre of a chipati and roll up; or fill with beansprouts (p 67) and yogurt (p 91); or coat with tomato paste and parmesan cheese (which has the highest concentration of calcium of any food: 1·2 per cent) and grill for just minutes; cover with grated raw carrots, turnip, or beetroot for light lunches; or tartex with lots of watercress for the day's supply of the B-complex family and cress's 5000 I.U.'s of carotene. Or be different. Roll up lightly cooked spinach, use seaweed, bundle fresh asparagus, smuggle salted plums into brown rice, hide away pieces of banana. Or make a variety, and bring out after an evening with friends.

Apple Strudel

If you want a real test of your abilities with flour, water and oil, this is it. It may not work the first time, but keep at it, for the results will gain the respect of even your great grandmother. There are two essential hints to follow. The dough must rest under a warm bowl for 30 min, the bowl being kept warm; and you must use your thumbs when pulling the pastry.

Make a well in a pile of 1lb (500g, 3 cups) of unbleached but white pastry flour. Put 1 tsp of fresh lemon juice (or apple vinegar) into the well, and sprinkle a bit of salt over the flour. Work 1 tbsp of butter into the pastry, crumbling with your fingers. Add WARM water to make a soft dough, more or less than 4oz (115ml, ½ cup) depending on the atmosphere. Smooth the dough into a ball, sprinkle with a little flour, and rest it under a warm bowl kept warm by replacing, or a hot towel. Cover the table (round ones are traditional) with a clean cloth (I keep a bit of sheeting for this) and sprinkle lightly with flour. Place the dough, the floured side down, on the table, and roll it out as far as it will go, making a big circle. Don't turn over and be careful not to tear. Brush with melted butter. Slip your hands under the pastry, lifting it up and down by flexing the back of your hands. After you are familiar with the bottom of the pastry, begin using your THUMBS to pull it out from the middle. Watch closely that you don't tear the pastry! Keep at it until you realize that the pastry is getting paper thin. When done, brush the pastry with more butter, and allow to rest and dry for 10 min. In the meantime, or with an assistant, grate from

12 to 15 eating apples, after coring. Place in a bowl, and sprinkle with allspice, or cloves and cinnamon. Add a bit of orange or lemon peel, and 2oz (60g, $\frac{1}{2}$ cup) ground hazel nuts. Put a thin layer of orange marmalade (the aged variety is best) on the pastry. Sprinkle sugar over the pastry, or put 8 tbsp of honey onto the apples if you wish sweetness. Take the apple mixture and spread out on half of the dough circle. Starting from the edge of the pastry, roll up like a jelly roll, leaving the unappled bit of pastry till last. Put on a baking sheet with the folded side at the bottom, and curl about like a horseshoe (inverted U). Prick lightly on top with a fork, dust with a little more spice, and bake in a moderate oven (375°F, 190°C, mark 5), until the pastry is puffed and golden (about 15-20 min). All sorts of fruits can go in along with a few apples—pears and grapes, or peaches, or currants, or freshly picked black-berries, or . . .

Norwegian Rusks

This delightful bread is served all over Norway with lots of yogurt and fresh berries all summer long, for breakfast, or for a late supper, or with one of the thick soups such as Rommegrot on p21. You will undoubtedly find your own way to use the rusks, such as in the Mushroom Casserole on p89.

1lb (500g, 3 cups) self-raising white flour
4oz (125g, 1 cup) brown sugar
4oz (125g, $\frac{1}{2}$ cup) melted butter or margarine
$\frac{1}{2}$pt (285ml, 1$\frac{1}{4}$ cups) single cream
$\frac{1}{2}$pt (285ml, 1$\frac{1}{4}$ cups) milk
1 tsp ground cardamom
$\frac{1}{2}$ yeast cake, or $\frac{1}{2}$ packet dried yeast ($\frac{1}{2}$oz, 15g)

Mix the flour and sugar together. Add yeast to a mixture of the milk, cream and melted butter (the milk and cream will then be slightly warm). Put the two sets of ingredients together, sprinkling the cardamom in as you mix. Form a ball of dough. Set aside in a covered bowl in a warm place and allow to rise for 2 hours. Knead out, and then shape into small rolls. Put them on an oiled baking sheet, and allow to rise again for 15-20 min (it will help to keep covered with a tea towel). Then bake at 375°F (190°C, mark 5) until crisp. Remove, let cool, and cut into halves which can then be dried a bit further by putting in the lowest temperature of the oven (200°F, 125°C, mark $\frac{1}{4}$) until lightly golden. Should make 4 dozen.

Gluten (Seitan)

If you want the protein of whole wheat flour (100 per cent) and less of the starch, or if you want to make a meatless cutlet, here's how:

1¼lb (625g, 4 cups) 100 per cent whole wheat flour
8oz (250g, 2 cups) unbleached white flour
1pt (570ml, 2½ cups) water
1-2 tsp sea salt

Combine the flours and add the water to make a dough. You may put the salt in at this point. Knead the dough for at least 20-30 min while winding down from the day, or while watching a sunset. Put the dough in a bowl and leave uncovered for about 30 min. Next pour 1qt (1l, 5 cups) water over the dough, and begin to knead the dough through the water. You will begin to extract a cream-coloured starch from the dough. Change the water (slightly warmed for comfort) several times, saving the changed water for soups or cooking beans. The dough gradually becomes more rubbery and little pieces of bran which turn up can be rinsed off if you wish. The final product, which does take a while to get to, is about half the volume of the flours. Chill it for awhile, and then cut with a knife into pieces. Cook in stews and soups, or press in some tarragon and lightly fry for a main protein dish.

SOY BEAN FLOURS

The soy bean, one of the richest sources of protein known, is gradually being introduced as a crop in both Sweden and England. As it yields approximately fourteen times more protein per acre than any animal, this is the main importance and value of soy bean to future ecology. The flour, as noted in our bread recipe (opposite), is valuable as a protein enhancer. It can have a bitter taste, and you may want to sweeten it if you use it elsewhere.

Soy Sweet

Indian cooks have long known soy flour (and chickpea or garbanzo flour) and knowing of its bitterness, have used it to make a dessert. Mix 4oz (125g, 1 cup) of soy flour with ½pt (285ml, 1¼ cups) condensed milk (or thick dried milk). Beat out any lumps, and add brown sugar if not sweet enough. Add raisins, pistachio nuts, orange and lemon peel, and a drop or two of mint syrup (p88). Cook for several minutes and then put in a container to set. Cut into squares. Protein for all, sweet enough for most. Delightful with cardamom tea (p93).

BREADS

Whole Wheat Honey Bread

16 fl oz (455ml, 2 cups) whole milk
3 tbsp unsalted butter
1 tbsp fine sea salt
8 tbsp honey, or 10 tbsp natural sugar
2 packets active dry yeast
5 tbsp lukewarm water
½ tsp fine brown sugar
1 lb 6oz (680g, 4 cups) unsifted whole wheat flour

Heat the milk just to boiling point, add the butter, salt, and honey and remove from the heat. Dissolve yeast in 5 tbsp lukewarm water with ½ tsp fine brown sugar. (More yeast may be used on cold days, or when faster rising is desired). Allow the yeast to soften for 5 min. Add the yeast mixture to the milk as soon as the milk has cooled to lukewarm (if the milk is too hot, the yeast will be killed). Add $\frac{3}{5}$ of the flour, and beat 300 strokes by hand, or 8 min at low speed with a mixer. Add the other $\frac{2}{5}$ of flour, and mix well. This has to be done by hand, unless your mixer has a bread hook. Put the dough on a floured board, knead until the dough no longer sticks to your hands and has developed a certain resilience—ie it should have enough body to spring back when touched firmly. Flour should be added during the kneading until the dough reaches this firm point. More flour may be needed in hot weather than in cold. Place the dough in a well oiled bowl, and turn about so that it is coated with oil. Cover with a towel sprinkled with warm water, and leave in a warm place to rise (such as on a storage heater or in a pan of warm water). When the dough has doubled in bulk, knead it back to its original size, cover, and allow to double in size again. Knead down a second time, but this time divide the dough into two parts, shape into 2 loaves, and place in lightly oiled and floured bread pans. Cover these with a towel and return to warm place until the dough has risen enough to lift the towel. Place in a preheated 375°F (190°C, mark 5) oven, and bake for 45 min, or until golden brown. Remove the bread from the pans at once, to prevent sticking.

Note: 3lb (1½kg) flour requires 1oz (30g) dry active yeast, which is equal to 2oz (60g) ordinary yeast. 6 tsp of dry active yeast is 1oz (30g). Use poppy, caraway or sesame seeds in and on the bread. Add dried gluten if you use heavy rye or buckwheat flours to prevent crumbling. Heavier doughs need to rest more. ¼ tsp toasted wheat germ per lb (500g) flour (raw germ will inhibit baking). Use 1 part soy flour to 20 parts wheat flour. Keep on kneading, it makes a lighter bread. Sandwiches are yours to construct.

Corn Bread

Serves 8

4oz (125g, 1 cup) stone ground yellow corn meal
4oz (125g, 1 cup) whole wheat flour or
unbleached white flour
1oz (30g) turbinado sugar
4 tsp cream of tartar
1 tbsp cornflour (corn starch)
8 fl oz (230ml, 1 cup) whole milk
2oz (60g, $\frac{1}{4}$ cup) fat (vegetable shortening)

Sift the dry ingredients together into a bowl, then add milk and blend in shortening. Beat until almost smooth, but leave a little lumpy. Pour batter into a greased 8 in square baking pan, and bake in a preheated 425°F (220°C, mark 7) oven for 20-25 min.

Treacle Bran Bread

An iron-rich bread that will give you even more benefit when combined with another protein dish. The darkness of the treacle (or blackstrap molasses) will mean watching the baking time carefully.

Warm 8 fl oz (230ml, 1 cup) milk with the same amount of yogurt in a saucepan and when baby bottle warm, remove from heat. Stir in 4 oz (125g, 1 cup) dried fruit, such as sultanas or chopped dates, and 8 oz (250g, 2 cups) whole bran cereal. Add 4 tbsp natural brown sugar, 2 tbsp vegetable oil and whip about. Meanwhile, sift 8oz (250g, 1$\frac{1}{2}$ cups) self-raising whole wheat flour with $\frac{1}{4}$ tsp fine sea salt, adding a dash of cream of tartar for lightness if you wish. Mix the flour with the liquids, and

beat together until completely combined. Turn batter into two oblong oiled and floured baking tins to a depth of 2in (5cm). Bake in a 350°F (175°C, mark 4) oven for 50 to 55 min.

Cheese Scones

Heat oven to 425°F (220°C, mark 7).

Sift together:
8oz (250g, 1$\frac{1}{2}$ cups) self-raising whole wheat flour
dash fine sea salt
sprinkle of coriander powder
$\frac{1}{2}$ tsp dry mustard
Rub or cut in:
1oz (30g) butter until the consistency
of breadcrumbs is reached
Grate:
4oz (125g) hard Cheddar cheese over the
flour mixture
Add:
$\frac{1}{4}$pt (140ml, $\frac{1}{2}$ cup) whole milk and form a
soft dough

Roll out on a floured bread board until about $\frac{1}{2}$in thick (1cm) and cut with a small glass that has been dipped in flour, or a metal cutter. Place on an oiled or teflon baking sheet and brush with milk to make smooth tops. Bake for about 12 min in preheated oven. Serve hot with a bit of cheese grated over the scones for glaze and taste. Serve as a bread, or use under the bean stew on p64.

PASTAS

If you don't have an Italian grandmother, or in my case, a Croatian great aunt, you may actually not yet know that pastas (spaghetti-like substances) are all from the same dough (or variations) and can happily be made at home.

Put 8oz (250g, 1½ cups) natural white flour into a large bowl, making a depression in the middle. Fill the well with 1½ tbsp olive oil, ½ tsp sea salt and 4 fl oz (115ml, ½ cup) of warm water (more or less), adding drops of water at a time while mixing the oil salt and flour. Make a firm ball of dough (touch the top of your nose to get the idea my aunt would say), and let it rest in a warm place in a bowl covered by another bowl. If you want pasta verde (the green variety) use well-drained, puréed spinach to make the dough, adding extra flour if the mixture is not firm enough. After the dough has had its nap, the fun begins, especially if you have a pasta machine to cut out fancy zig-zags, and cartwheels, as the illustration shows. If not don't despair, and do one of the following.

The simplest is just to take pinches of dough off the ball at the time and let them dry for several hours (or all day in the sun) on a clean cloth or paper. This is the thumbprint variety that bambinos begin with. (A dough made with whole wheat flour is ideal for this pasta.) Cut strips from a rolled out dough to make fettuccine, or make 12-18in rectangles (4in wide) for lasagne, which is especially good with the verde (green) variety. For spaghetti you will need either a keen eye and a sharp knife, or a special sieve or pasta machine. Cook all the above in a large pot with plenty of water, preferably infused with basil and thyme, or oregano and onion bits. Add tsps of olive oil to the water to prevent the pastas from sticking together and making lumps. Lasagne is particularly inclined to gossip. It bears repeating that the best pastas are not overcooked, and so remain chewy or 'al dente'.

Pastas love sauces made from tomatoes, or just plain butter with a bit of garlic and pepper (as in the case of the fettuccine).

Tomato Sauce

A pan full of deseeded and drained tomatoes, preferably the Italian plum variety, 2 tsp basil, 2 tsp thyme, 1 tsp vegetable salt, ½lb (250g) chopped cleaned fresh mushrooms is cooked over a low heat for hours until bubbly sauce is cooking, thickening the sauce with a bit of removed sauce blended into some flour and then returned to the pot. ½lb (250g) of cheese grated into the sauce makes it particularly nice. *Note:* Some varieties of pasta like to have tbs of soy flour (or other egg substitute) added in the making stage for improved texture and pliability.

Ravioli

There are various ways to make raviolis, as both the Chinese and the Italians have been at it for centuries. One simple way is to take the recipe for pie crust (p 51) and use it to produce two circles or squares of dough. Roll out as thin as you can, and brush with butter. Allow to rest a few minutes, while you make the fillings. Italian soft cheeses such as fontina, ricotta, cottage cheese or cream cheese with dill rubbed in; peanut butter and cheddar, sufficient for 1 tsp per ravioli. The idea is to put the dobs of filling evenly, but about ¾in (2cm) apart (all sides) on one of the pieces of dough, and then lay the other dough across the top. Using the 'bumps' as your guide, use a pastry cutter to cut squares about each filling. Crimp the edges together with a fork or your fingers, and put in a moderate oven (375°F, 190°C, mark 5) on to an oiled baking sheet and dry out for 10 min. Allow to cool down. Make up a pan of tomato sauce (see p59) and drop the raviolis into it when bubbling. Remove from heat and let cool a bit, then serve with green pepper salad (p 28) and bowls of grated cheese.

Spinach Lasagne

Before we begin you should think of lasagne making and 7 other people at the same time. There is not really such a thing as a small lasagne if you go to the time and trouble. And love for complicated food gives you the chance not only to show off your herbs, but to think about what is important as you make up a communal dish. Eastern teachers advise the saying of prayers while cooking; lasagne entered into in the proper mood, is not unrelated to other types of devotion. Now then, food philosophy having been stated, please ease your mind by thinking about the lasagne as a stack of huge cheese sandwiches, made with the lasagne pasta described overleaf. The illustration is carefully designed to show you the stacking process. The most important piece of advice is to drain all the ingredients unless you have the special lasagne casserole with the two layers, one with holes in it. The best textured lasagnes are those with a firmness that comes from long cooking, but with fresh spinach, too much cooking destroys the vitamins and iron.

Gather together 20 or more sheets of cooked lasagne verde pasta (or plain lasagne if eggless); 2pt (1l, 5 cups) tomato sauce (see p59); 3-4lb (2kg) fresh or defrosted frozen spinach (or other green leaves if desired); 2lb (1kg) drained ricotta, cottage or brineless Feta (Greek) cheese; 1lb (500g) rennet-free Cheddar cheese; several fresh spearmint or peppermint sprigs, and several oz of black and green pitted olives, ½lb (250g) cut, cooked and drained mushrooms.

Take a large baking dish (the length of the lasagne) and hopefully several inches deep. If not deep enough a collar of heavy foil can be made, as the illustration shows, being careful to leave overlap on the sides, as one of the functions of the foil is to help lift the lasagne out. This means that basically you are making a topless box of foil, to set inside the baking dish or pan (bread tins will bake one width of lasagne at a time, but you will need several of them for this recipe).

Spread a thin layer of sauce across the bottom of the dish, then a layer of cooked lasagne pasta, then sauce, cheese, mushrooms, sauce, lasagne pasta, sauce, freshly cooked and completely drained spinach, a mint sprig, sauce, cheese, olives (pitted), sauce, lasagne pasta, and so on, until you have 5 or more layers, with pasta, sauce and cheese on the top. Alternate the soft and hard cheeses. Bake for 20-30 min at 350°F (180°C, mark 4). Remove from oven, and slit the foil in the bottom, lifting lasagne gently to let any accumulated liquids drain. Return to oven, adding more cheese to the top, and any decorations. (Grill the top for a minute if your oven has a grill.) Take out of oven, get someone to help you lift the lasagne out of the pan, fold back the foil, and tell the crowd to come on in. Serve with this year's white grape juices, and a dandelion salad (p 88). And give yourself a degree in culinary art.

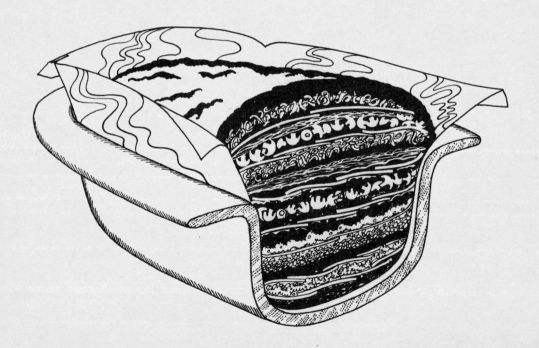

PROTEIN COUNT

Throughout this book, from recipes for how to make gluten to lentil and pea soups, from chili to bean sprouts, homemade cheeses and breads to sweets such as rommegrot and breakfasts of muesli and oatmeal, the silent concern has been to choose those dishes rich in vitamins, minerals, and PROTEIN. But protein is a group name (like Harris) and the real pleasure is getting to know the individuals (the amino acids). For amino acids combine and recombine in endless chains to make up protein groups, and to build up even greater structures such as you, yourself. But the proteins have to be digested and broken down into amino acids, so that the new proteins can be formed. Which is why, nutritionally speaking, it's perfectly sensible to be a vegetarian. Eliminate the innocent animal in between you and the amino acids in the soybean, and you efficiently go about utilizing that soybean. Human milk is assumed to be the norm, and the chart below has been especially constructed from research figures to show you how various vegetarian amino acid sources compare to human milk. For purposes of reassuring your omnivorous friends that your diet is healthy, flesh is given as well. The eight that your body doesn't make itself are emphasized. One last point: amino acids appear to be most useful in combinations—hence the continuous mixing of one source rich in leucine (cheese) with methionine (brazil nuts) gives best results.

AMINO ACIDS PER GRAM NITROGEN	Human Milk	Cow Milk and Cheese	Brown Rice	Brown 100% Wheat Flour	Brazil Nuts	Cashews	Soy Beans	Lentils	French Beans (Green Beans)	Meat and Meat Products
Valine	0·39	0·44	0·39	0·27	0·30	0·46	0·33	0·35	0·41	0·33
Leucine	0·59	0·62	0·51	0·40	0·43	0·44	0·48	0·44	0·51	0·49
Isoleucine	0·35	0·39	0·30	0·24	0·23	0·35	0·33	0·33	0·38	0·22
Threonine	0·28	0·29	0·22	0·18	0·16	0·21	0·25	0·23	0·29	0·28
Methionine	0·13	0·15	0·13	0·10	0·32	0·10	0·08	0·04	0·08	0·15
Lysine	0·39	0·49	0·26	0·17	0·16	0·23	0·40	0·39	0·44	0·51
Phenylalanine	0·25	0·32	0·29	0·29	0·21	0·27	0·31	0·26	0·39	0·26
Tryptophan	0·10	0·09	0·09	0·18	0·07	0·14	0·09	0·05	0·08	0·08

Carli's Bean Stew

For best results soak the beans for at least 24 hours. This keeps the cooking time down. So soak 1 small handful each of: soy beans, red beans, black beans, haricot beans (or blackeyed peas), lentils, and split green peas (after rinsing). Add sufficient water to cover again the following day, and bring to a boil in a large heavy pan with a lid. Add 2 tbsp vegetable oil to prevent sticking. Reduce heat once boiling commences, and keep just high enough to keep the pot simmering. Check after 45 min to make sure that the lentils are not sticking to the bottom, and then every 10 min until beans are soft but still crunchy. Turn heat off, and cut up 2 large onions, 2 leeks, and 4 medium carrots. Add to beans with a bit of butter (they may be sautéed for several min before adding). Spices such as a clove of garlic, 2 tsp paprika, 2 tsp soy sauce, a dash of cumin and a sprinkle of tarragon may be added as well. Then wait for 15 min just while the beans and vegetables merge flavours. Serve with sour cream and a quarter of a lemon per person. The cheapest complete protein dish of all. Serves 4-6.

MEAT SUBSTITUTES

Various commercially prepared 'meat substitutes' (which as you learned from the protein chart is quite a natural range) were originally dreamed up for appeasing transition diets. Some, usually with egg whites, are currently appearing in even the supermarkets as additives for hamburger, and budget stretchers. Read the labels—some are as full of chemicals as house paint. Still, some are old products by reliable firms and can be used with appropriate spices to hasten a meal, fool friends, or make mother happy by having 'turkey' with your Christmas dinner.

Traditional yeast products such as the vegetable patés made by Tartex, and marvellous Marmite, are truly superior (Marmite's food values are even listed in charts—123mg Calcium, 7mg Iron, 5.2mg B_2, and a whopping 59mg nicotine acid.)

Cutlets

Make your own by shaping gluten (p 56) and frying in a light oil with thyme and tarragon and a dash of paprika. Soy sauce for added flavour. Or make up nut loaves (p 83), bean loaves (p 70), or fry a bit of to fu (p 67).

Groundnut Stew

A West African speciality is easily adapted for use with any of the new meatless meats that are currently on the market. Be sure that they are also eggless.

Serves 4

In a large frying pan, cook 1½lb (750g) dried soy meat (or our gluten, p56) until tender. Next fry it lightly in oil with 2 medium onions and 2 sliced green peppers until the onions and peppers are cooked. Meanwhile put 1lb (500g) unskinned (but shelled) peanuts through a nut grinder or the blender. Add to soy, and dash on red chili powder. Blend in a small 2oz (60g) can of tomato paste and sufficient water to make the whole of stew consistency. Take off heat, and garnish with 2-3 cut up medium sized tomatoes, and tbsp of sour cream. More chili can be put on at the table if desired.

West African Millet

Per serving:

Cook 2oz (60g, ½ cup) millet flour in 8 fl oz (230ml, 1 cup) boiling water and stir until it becomes completely brown and partially set, about 15 min. Can be fried in butter or peanut oil. Serve with salad for a quick lunch, or as a side dish to Groundnut Stew.

Were a Stuffing Designed for Peppers

Raw or grilled for several min until soft (coat with olive oil to protect the skin), large sweet green or golden peppers obviously have cavities that need filling. One of the more exquisite is a blend of 2oz (60g) pineapple cream cheese, 1oz (30g) pistachio kernels, and sufficient whole wheat bread crumbs to give texture. Or for heartiness, mix together several oz fried mushrooms, celery leaves, 2oz (60g) cottage cheese, and 3oz (90g) cooked brown rice or kasha.

Or Designed for Tomatoes

Cut out a 'cap' from the top end, core out the seeds, and fill with a cut up baked or boiled potato that has been dressed with ½ tsp mustard, a few dill seeds, a dash of olive oil and a squeeze of lemon (ie potato salad). Garnish with chopped chives. Serve cold, or grill. Small tomatoes can have their centres filled with nut butters (p83) for appetizers.

EAT INDIAN

CURRIES

No, Virginia, there is not a curry plant. So, Virginia, you can have all the fun of making up your own, unless you get a supply of privately-blended powders from a fakir of your choice (such as the illustrious one who draws for this book and who likes to blend his own). The point being that commercial blends are too indelicate for much of the best of Indian cookery, which does rival the French, Italian, and Chinese for gourmet status, the all night joint down the road to the contrary. Moreover, the best Indian restaurants blend their own. To give examples. All curry blends start with turmeric and a hot or a sweet paprika. Sweets and vegetables benefit from cloves, cinnamon, cardamom, saffron and various green leaves mixed with the sweet paprika. Potatoes and other roots such as carrots are treated to a bit of cumin, black pepper, and a blend of sweet and hot peppers. Oils can be added to make curry pastes, and crushed fruits such as dates and sultanas make for thick consistencies. Four thousand or more years of vegetarian tradition are yours to explore. Don't forget to keep the grinds mildish though, as too much pepper in even a mango pickle makes for indigestion and an over-stimulated mental state. Raitas (p35) help to maintain the balance.

Now then, some samples:

Bombay Potatoes

Mix 1 tsp turmeric with $\frac{1}{2}$ tsp hot paprika, a dash of cloves, a dash of cardamom, freshly grated ginger and sea salt—enough curry for two servings of cut up boiled potatoes in their skins. Mix in chopped green pepper and add butter.

Dahl (Lentils)

Mix 1 tsp turmeric with 1 tsp hot paprika, a grating of fresh ginger, several dashes of powdered clove, and garlic. Put aside. Cook $\frac{1}{2}$lb (250g) lentils and $\frac{1}{4}$lb (125g) raisins or currants in about 1pt water (570ml, $2\frac{1}{2}$ cups) until lentils become soft. Add $\frac{1}{2}$lb (250g) fresh or frozen peas, and stir in the curry.

Onions Bhajee

Mix 1 tsp turmeric with 2 tsp hot paprika, dashes of powdered cloves, a tsp tip of saffron, chili powder or liquid to taste. Blend into 4oz (125g, 1 cup) whole wheat flour. Add sufficient water to make a heavy paste and roll in 5 medium sized onions cut into small wedges. Make into small patties, and then deep fry.

Curried Fresh Fruit

Mix 1 tsp turmeric, 1 tsp sweet paprika, $\frac{1}{2}$ tsp powdered cardamom, dash of rose water, and cinnamon. Add to slices of fresh pears or apricots. Serve with cream.

EAT CHINESE

CHINESE NOTES

The art of Chinese cookery is a subject for books of great length, so let it just be suggested here that the Chinese Buddhists developed the most luscious, delicate and nutritious ways of preparing foods. Among the treasures well worth knowing are tools such as the 'wok', an inverted cone skillet which allows (most scientifically) a small amount of fuel to heat a large surface evenly and quickly so that vegetables can be steam fried in just minutes, flavours intact, and nutrition sealed in. Ingredients such as waterlily stems, fresh ginger, snowpea pods, bamboo shoots, bean threads and mung bean sprouts, and the development of soy bean cheeses (below), soy sauces (miso) are worth the trouble of tracking down. Don't use MSG—mono sodium glutinate.

Soy Bean Cheese (To Fu)

Use either tinned soy bean milk, or full fat soy bean powder (not defatted). In the latter case, mix 6oz (180g, 1 cup) soy flour with 8 fl oz (230ml, 1 cup) of cold water, and pour into 20 fl oz (570ml, 2½ cups) of boiling water. Then heat either the tinned milk, or the made milk, in a double boiler, and allow to come to a boil. Add the juices of 2 lemons, and just stir enough to blend thoroughly. Let the mixture cool slowly in the top pan, keeping it in the hot water. When it coagulates, pour through a fine cheese cloth, or through a cheese press if you have one. Squeeze any excess water out. You can dust with spices, or grate on ginger. Wrap in a cheese cloth, and store (covered with water) in a refrigerator.

CHINESE BEAN SPROUTS

After growing your own from soy or mung beans, you may like to cook them lightly for some cold winter day. Do cook lightly, or the whole struggle to have greens in the winter will be to no avail. Sautée a handful per serving in just the barest bit of sesame oil until sprouts start to get greener (a minute or two at most) and then add 1 tsp of water, cover, and remove from heat. Grate on a bit of ginger, add some ginko beans (or other soft bean), or a handful of grated carrot or turnip. Return to the heat, and cook 1 min longer. You can add water chestnuts if you have a tin, or slices of celery. An aged soy sauce or miso (from the macrobiotic store) is an ideal 'sauce'. A dish low in calories, high in food value. (See p38.)

Spring Mould

If you have seen this delicate protein and mineral-rich dish, which hovers somewhere between a sweet, a vegetable, and a salad, in the windows of Chinese stores, chances are it will be in various shades and colours due to food colouring. If your taste runs, as does mine, to the colours that Nature gave it in the first place, read on:

4oz (125g, 1 cup) cooked green peas, puréed
4oz (125g, 1 cup) cooked water chestnuts, puréed
4oz (125g, 1 cup) Chinese walnuts, pulverized or finely chopped
6 tbsp honey or 6 tbsp ground sesame seeds (gomasio) and salt
6 tbsp vegetable oil
little water

This takes three small bowls, one for each ingredient. Cream in 2 tbsp honey or gomasio, and a little water into each of the three ingredients, until fluffy. Sautée each ingredient in a frying pan (skillet) with 2 tbsp of oil for 5 min, and when done place on a platter, separating into 2 or more piles each of pea, chestnut, and walnuts. Mould together so that the colours alternate and make stripes. Paint the whole with a bit of water and oil to give a sheen, and after allowing to stand a few minutes, serve. Parsley or mint can be added to the peas, nutmeg or paprika to the chestnuts, and cloves or cinnamon to the walnuts, or suit your own palate. If chilled, good in the evening. Decorate with a pastry tube of cream cheese.

Tempuras

Tempura is really the name of a way of life once you get into it, but the word tells of its Japanese origins: something dipped into a rice flour batter and deep fried in a wok (curved steel bowl) for just minutes or even seconds until the dough is crisped. The nutritional advantage is that the dough preserves the vegetables, the cooking time is short, and the vegetable does have time to loose its raw taste. As commercial tempura batter mixes use egg whites, mix your own from rice flour, water, several tbsp of soy flour, and a bit of soy sauce or paste. Then dip parsley (for snowy trees of vitamin A), green beans, onion quarters, sliced sweet potatoes, sliced, salted and drained aubergines (egg plant), whole or cross-sliced mushrooms, carrot sticks, celery tops etc in the batter. Use tongs to avoid tempured fingers as all the above are then dipped into 3-4 in of hot oil until just crisp.

Sar Hor Fun (Fresh Rice Noodles)

Eventually, if you do much Chinese cookery you will have to invest in some of the utensils such as the mortar and pestle and the woven bamboo basket. I mention the latter two because they are essential for the making of these Sar Hor Fun noodles, unless you care to improvise. The noodles, once made have to be steamed, and a small round basket is just the thing. I have made them in a wire net used by some to steam vegetables, but they were difficult to cook properly without becoming gummy. A blender that grinds can be used instead of a mortar and pestle. Needless to say, noodles are made in huge quantities, but will keep in the fridge.

Wash about 4lb (2kg, 8 cups) rice (brown short-grain) until clear of all dust. Put in a pot, cover with water and leave overnight, or for a day. After draining, grind in mortar (or blend) until of a fine, clear consistency. Empty into a large, deep container of water and allow the rice to settle in the bottom. Place a muslin cloth over the bamboo tray and scoop the wet rice mixture onto the muslin. Placing it over a large container of boiling water, steam the rice for 10 min. Turn out onto a cool metallic or stone surface and knead into a roll. Allow to rest a bit, and then cook in a pot of boiling liquid for 5 min. Delicious with fresh green cabbage, or as a dessert with apricots or peaches, or cherries.

Sakura's Vegetable Skiyaki

In the middle of Texas, of all places, there is a Japanese restaurant, and the wonderful ladies who used to serve there produced vegetarian delights time and time again in response to just a bit of manners upon our part—such as telephoning in advance, coming at one end of the peak hours, and bringing more than one vegetarian.

Cut 1lb (500g) of fresh to fu (Japanese bean-curd cheese—the tinned and dried varieties are marginally good) into cubes and marinate with miso (aged soy sauce). Take 6oz (180g) of Chinese pea pods, fresh or frozen; several oz of mushrooms, ideally the black tree mushrooms, or the cloud variety, fresh or tinned or re-constituted dried ones; 4 oz (125g, 1 cup) bean sprouts (see p67); 1 tin bamboo shoots 4 oz (125g) (unless you grow your own); a large frying pan (skillet) full of soy oil and soy sauce in equal parts, heated until water sizzles. Place each of the ingredients into its own space, and bubble cook for 5-7 min. You can add parsley, slices of green pepper, fresh green onions sliced lengthwise, and even bean threads in the last minutes. When all green and gleeful, drain and serve at once. Great with vegetables tempura (see p68). *Note:* Cubes of other soft cheeses can be substituted, especially Cheshire. If you can get lotus roots, or stems, have powdered burdock root for colouring, and like to grate a bit of fresh ginger, good for you. Fresh spinach can be used.

Blackeyed Peas (Beans)

Although the delicate flavours of this shy bean are best appreciated when it is just freshly shelled, or even in the frozen form, it is still quite sweet flavoured even after being dried. It must be soaked for at least 8 hours, but a longer soaking will improve the taste (as with all beans). Its slight wild flavour is enhanced by using tarragon leaves in the soaking and cooking water (same water). Cook until soft but still crunchy, and serve as is, for a solo protein item. Gourmet status can be attained by stirring in one of the French cream cheeses such as chived boursin.

Bean Loaf

Mash or grind cooked beans until pulpy, blend in 2oz (60g, ½ cup) whole wheat flour and 2-3oz (60-90g) cottage or farmers' cheese. Add several oz (50-100g, ½-1 cup) vegetables such as parsnips, carrots, leeks, turnips, boiled sweet onions, or corn off the cob. Mash all together, and form in a casserole or loaf pan, and bake at 350°F (180°C, mark 4) until firm and lightly browned. So you have a bean loaf, and yes, other beans can be used (soy can be bitter by itself though).

Banana Nut Risotto

In preparing properly, eliminate any potential mush by using only firm bananas which will absorb only so much of the spice, and will thus remain sweet and distinct. To avoid mess, don't overcook the brown rice. Forget about the enriched white rices and their dustings of vitamin and/or milk powder. Frying in vegetable oil and not butter gives you an unsaturated oil, and no danger of black scorching. Finally, red pepper or mild paprika is a rich source of vitamins A and C. They should be used as a tickle to the palate and not as air-hammers on the stomach. Cumin powder, and an Indian leaf called methi can be used for the authentic touch.

Cook 4oz (125g, 1 cup) brown rice per serving (see p 49), plus one extra portion for seconds per hungry guest. Infuse the cooking water with the methi leaves, paprika, and cumin. When the rice is almost cooked, stir in handfuls of cashew nuts, peanuts, walnut meats, or almonds (which the guests can shell for the best freshness). Sprinkle on red pepper to taste, and stir in tbsp of olive oil. Turn out into an oiled fry pan (skillet), and fry the rice and nuts for just a few min to get a better texture. Onions can be fried along. Then on a large platter, build layers of rice, slices of green bananas, rice, bananas, and so on until you've used up the rice. Garnish the whole with a few grapes, and rings of green pepper. Fun.

CHEESE PLEASE

An assumption that has been running through this book has been that there would come a time when the way in which cheese is made would have to be discussed. So here we are at the most delightful of dairy products and the unsavoury subject of rennet. Rennet coagulates milk (in your stomach as well) and makes possible the formation of cheese curds. It is unfortunately still extracted from the stomachs of calves, and while it seems to be but a trace quantity in the finished cheese, it has been there, and many strict vegetarians feel that it is best to forego cheese except for the rennet-free varieties such as cream cheese and cottage cheese, or those that we have gathered in the next pages. Most cheeses can be made without rennet, and some are available through health food sources. A few commercially available cheeses such as gjetost, certain Swiss cheeses, varieties of parmesan, and farm cheeses such as the boursins of France, are frequently rennet-free. There are a number of cheese encyclopedias that give the process used for every cheese. If you find this too fussy, or are prepared to think of rennet as a micro-organism, or can find good sources, you may want to build a card index file on the harmonious affinities of various cheeses you come to know. This research is so that you can build what the French call 'Plateaux de Fromage' which should have one goat cheese, a veined cheese (the veins are from various moulds often of the penicillin family), a hard cheese and a decorative cheese. The illustration shows a French banon (wrapped in chestnut leaves, a veined Stilton, a Swiss, and a soft grape cheese which gets its flavour from the grape seeds and pulp that are pressed onto its sides. The protein and calcium of cheese are not affected by heat.

Hungarian Bread and Cheese

It's not the bread that's Hungarian but the way in which the cheese is prepared. This dish goes by the name of Liptoi.

Blend:

½lb (250g) cottage cheese
¼lb (125g) dairy butter
½ tsp dried mustard
½ tsp caraway seeds
2 tsp chopped fresh chives
2 tsp small or chopped capers
dash of paprika

Spread on homemade bread (see p57) or rye crackers or slices of pumpernickle. Makes a good hors d'oeuvre or a lunch for taking to work or when travelling.

Homemade Jugoslavian Cheese (Kaimar)

Using flattish soup bowls, fill them with whole milk, and leave in a warm place for 2-3 hours. This 'turns' the milk. Carefully remove the layer of cream that forms with a skimming ladle, and place in another bowl with the tiniest bit of salt. Repeat, as is possible if you get more cream. Makes a cheese somewhat like cottage cheese, and if allowed to ferment will develop a great pungency. Goat or sheep milk is fine if you wish. Use the whey to make a soup.

Indian Cheese (Paneer)

Bring 3pt (1½l, 7½ cups) of full milk to boil, remove from heat, and whip in 1 tsp powdered alum (which you can order from a chemist shop or from a friend in a laboratory). Place pan back on heat, and stir mixture until the milk curdles and separates from the whey. Drain into a large strainer, and then put curds into a muslin or cheese cloth bag. Squeeze out the extra whey and mould by pressing into any wooden box that has a top smaller than the sides which can be pressed in on top. Dust with saffron for a deep yellow colour, and serve with curried peas. Can be grilled in cubes, or sautéed; and with rosewater, brown sugar syrups, cardamom, and walnuts, makes a sweet.

Balkan Cheese Sticks

Prepare a pastry from:

4oz (125g, 1 stick) butter
8oz (250g, 1½ cups) whole wheat flour
8oz (250g, 2 cups) grated sharp cheese

Let grow cold (refrigerate in summer) for 15-20 min (when a sheen will appear) and then roll out quite thin. Cut into finger-length strips, as wide as your small finger. Twist together two strips into a braid. Sprinkle with poppy or caraway or sesame seeds, dust with paprika and sprinkle with more grated cheese. Bake in a 375°F (190°C, mark 5) oven until crisp and snappy (about 10 min).

Cheesey Turnip Roll

Turnips, or sweet
swedes, or scottish neaps,
are usually found mashed, and
hopefully with a bit of butter and
nutmeg. Or you can cut thick slices, parboil them for a minute or so, and then grill
until cooked but still firm. Find a heavy piece of
string and knot one end with a bit of stick in the knot.
Then thread the slices of turnip on the string, dashing cloves
on one slice, and nutmeg on another, adding bits of carrot, or
the big flat caps of giant mushrooms, and whole sides of green pepper
and wedges of tomato and slices of precooked aubergine (egg plant) and
so on and on until you have a huge roll. Roll the whole in a frying pan full of
melted cheeses, and then dip the cheese-coated roll into a pan full of bread
and biscuit crumbs. Roll over and over, picking up what you can, dipping
back into the cheese, and into the crumbs again, then lay the whole
on an oiled baking tin and tie a knot in the other end and put a
stick in it to hold the whole together, basting with a
bit of soy oil and sauce for flavour, and maybe
bits of finely chopped green onions. Bake at
400°F (205°C, Mark 6) for about 30 min, or
until the crumbs start to get overly-
anxious to burn or to go sliding off
to the bottom of the pan with
the cheese and make
a mess. Remove
from oven
and eat.

FONDUES

Assuming that your vegetarianism excludes alcohol, and that you don't trust it to burn off when cooking; or assuming that you happen to like the delicate flavour of natural juices and not some heavy batch of alcoholic esters, then you can use either red or white grape juices in any recipe involving your fondue pan. Cheese fondues, chocolate or carob fondues, fruit fondues, and so on. The word is from the French *fondre* which means to melt.

Grape Juice Fondue

8oz (250g) grated Emmenthal or grated Gruyere are mixed with 4oz (125g) grated strong Cheddar and 1 tbsp unbleached white flour. Melt in a heavy pot, preferably a ceramic one (the metal ones are for meats and operate differently) in about ½pt (285ml, 1¼ cups) unsweetened grape juice. For best results, heat the juice first. When the mixture is bubbly transfer pot to a stand with a candle to keep it warm. Using fondue forks if you have them, and regular ones if you don't, skewer cubes of bread, and pieces of fruit (such as apples and pineapple) and dip. Let cool a moment to prevent burnt mouths! One person known to us even enjoys dipping fresh nuts, water chestnuts, pieces of green pepper, cubes of hard cheeses, and slightly cooked mushrooms. Rather intelligent bloke.

Sour Cream Fondue

Another fondue with a satin texture and a pleasant mild flavour. Quantities for 4.

8oz (250g) Gloucester or aged Cheddar cheese
1 tsp whole wheat flour
½pt (300cc, 1¼ cups) sour or cultured cream
1 tsp chopped chives
dash coriander

Grate the cheese coarsely and put it in the fondue pot. Sprinkle the flour over and mix. Add the cream, chives and coriander to the cheese and heat. Stir continuously until the cheese is melted and the mixture is bubbling. Add a dash of soy sauce for character if you wish. Serve with whole wheat bread or toast cut into large pieces.

SWEETS AND PUDDINGS

Munchies

If your dentist is as pleasant as mine he will not mind that just now and again you have a craving for something to munch upon, such as warm nutmegged milk and munchies at bedtime, for insomnia; or munchies for taking to work or school (the protein content along with the natural sugar guarantee a sustaining bit of nutrition). The 'additives'—the fruits, nuts, carob bits, coconut, yeast, and even wheat germ—are additional goodness.

Cream 6oz (180g, ¾ cup) vegetable shortening (or margarine, not butter) into 6oz (180g, 1 cup) dark brown natural sugar. Add 4oz (125g, 1 cup) unbleached self-raising flour, 1oz (30g, ¼ cup) yeast flakes or wheat germ,

and 1 tsp allspice and a dash of powdered clove. Blend all ingredients together until soft mixture is formed. To obtain a slightly wet mixture, add 2 fl oz (60ml, ¼ cup) apple juice or the same of sweet milk. Let mixture rest and heat oven to 350°F (180°C, mark 4). Squeeze in 12oz (375g, 3 cups) oatmeal flakes by hand (kiddies love this stage) and 2oz (60g, ½ cup) each of sultanas (or mixed dried fruit) and carob bits. When mixture is worked together put tsp-sized rounded bits onto oiled baking sheets and bake for 12-15 min. Produces about 4 dozen munchies. Store in a tight jar to keep crisp, or leave in a bowl if slight softening is desired. Lock in the vault if anyone is dieting.

Indian Sweets

Some Indian sweets are too sugary for Western taste, and a few are too bitter (those made from green soybean flour). Most require special flours, spices, or techniques, but happily not all. Hot or cold, newly made or several days old, the delight described below is the elegant equivalent of the old nursery rhyme about peas porridge.

Infuse several cups of water with cardamom seeds, cinnamon sticks, cloves, and either a star anise or two or aniseed. When the infusion has boiled for 10 min reduce heat and simmer with 8 tbsp honey added, or 10 tbsp dark brown sugar (or if you like treacle or blackstrap molasses add about 8 tbsp or to taste). Strain out the spices, and for each cup of liquid stir in 3 tbsp semolina or cream of wheat. Stir until mixture is thick and bubbly, adding another tbsp of semolina if additional thickening is needed. Remove from heat when almost solid in consistency, and stir in several handfuls of sultanas, or currants, or cut up dried apricots, or dried berries. Grate a bit of orange or tangerine peel over the top, and decorate the whole with slices of apple, or orange peel or, to be truly authentic, sheets of the silver foil that are sold at Indian speciality shops. Your Indian friends will appreciate a syrup of honey and rosewater poured over the top. Serve with marsala tea (p 94).

Carrot Cake

If you are serving this dish to non-initiated friends, it may be wise to mention the main ingredients after the praise has been given—mental blocks about carrots run second only to spinach!

Preheat the oven to 350°F (180°C, mark 4). An even heat is essential for thorough cooking of this delicious sweet.

Cream $\frac{1}{4}$lb (125g, 1 stick) butter or margarine. When light and fluffy, blend in 6oz (200g, 1 cup) demerara sugar and 3-4 tbsp milk. Stir rapidly until all is liquid, then sift in 10oz (300g, $2\frac{1}{2}$ cups) brown self-raising flour. Let rest and grate 12oz (375g, 3 cups) raw carrots into a large bowl. Sprinkle $\frac{1}{2}$-1 tsp each of powdered cloves, cinnamon and cardamom (or allspice and mace) over the carrots, making sure all are coated. Add in flour mixture and mix in the carrots with the fingers. Bake in 2 bread tins or one 8in by 8in baking tin—having oiled and floured the tins—for about 45-50 min or slightly longer in chilly, damp weather. A knife should be inserted and come out clean if the cake is done. Serve with whipped thick cream as a topping if you're indulging.

Funeral Pie

This unusually named tart comes from the Moravian and Shaker areas of Eastern America. There is no mystery about the name as the concoction was invariably to be found at gatherings of the family, one such occasion being the loss of some relative. It is so healthy that it is easy to believe that it was not the simplicity and the colouring of the pie that were its attractions, but its sustaining strength.

Use either a shell made from pastry or crumbled digestive biscuits patted into a pie tin and held into place with melted butter. Soak 1lb (500g, 3 cups) seeded raisins or sultanas, 8oz (250g, 1 cup) of natural brown sugar, 2oz (60g, $\frac{1}{2}$ cup) whole wheat flour, 1 tbsp vinegar, bits of butter and dashes of cinnamon. Soak the raisins in water for $2\frac{1}{2}$-3 hours, drain and mix with sugar, flour and vinegar. Put into the pastry shell with spoonfuls of butter and sprinkle with cinnamon. The pie can either be cooked open or be covered with a second crust or more crumbled biscuits. Bake at moderate temperature 400°F (200°C, mark 6) for about 35 min. Check the pie at that point and if it needs yet more baking leave it in the oven for another 5-10 min. Serve as is, or top with cream.

Nut Brittle

No Southerner in the United States would ever believe that his favourite 'candy' came from China, nor would the Chinese friends of mine who first gave me this recipe recognize the sad, dyed and tasteless thing their favourite sweet has become after commercialization. Here is the original recipe for you to get acquainted with. Honey and molasses can be used as the sweetener, but as they both vary so much as to water content, it is difficult to judge the quantities.

Make a syrup from 8oz (250g, 1 cup) brown sugar, 3 tbsp of vinegar, and 1 tbsp water. Cook until the syrup thickens and will make a brittle strand when tested in a cup of cold water (250°F on cooking thermometer, 125°C). Oil a baking tin with peanut oil and cover with unskinned (but shelled) peanuts or any other nut. Pour the syrup over the nut, flattening out evenly. Before the brittle is completely cold, cut into any shapes. Store in a tight container, or it will soften and even mould.

APPLES

Apple Butter

I have a friend who can't buy fresh farm produce without letting his common sense go by the board. Bargains appeal, the smells entice, and so he ends up with baskets of freshly picked apples each autumn. As happens, he eats only an apple or two at a time, and strudel making is time consuming, and . . . You guessed it, the apples begin to give signs of turning brown. So if that's your story as well here's the answer.

10lb (5kg) cooking apples
12pt (5l) apple cider (non-alcoholic)
4lb (2kg) dark brown sugar
2 heaped tbsp each of cinnamon, allspice, and mace (or cloves)

You need lots of time to peel all the apples, and perhaps you should throw a peeling party. Cook the cut up apples in the cider with the spices for 10 min or until tender. Put the lot through a colander and return to pan, adding the sugar. Cook until the apples become a soft paste, stirring from time to time to prevent burning. Bottle and distribute to your friends or store in dark coolness.

Note: Rosehips can be added for colour and vitamin C, but only in the last min.

The Baked Apple

Perhaps you simply want a sensible dessert, or a quick working lunch. Then it's baked apples with or without stuffings. They can be baked *au naturel*, but extra energy and nutrition can be slipped in by:

Coring the apples and filling the cavity with a mixture of two-thirds of your favourite nut butter, and one-third seeded currants or sultanas (for iron). Variations are fun, especially if a child is home to make them: fresh grapes; a mixture of sesame seed tahini and tamari soy sauce; a mixture of pineapple, mint leaves and a dash of cloves; pinenuts (pinolas) and honey; or slices of block deseeded dates with a dab of cream cheese on top.

Place filled apples in a shallow pan to keep oven clean, and collect drippings. Bake at a moderate temperature (350°F, 180°C, mark 4) for 20 min. Wrapped in tin foil the apples bake more quickly, or on the edge of an open fire or bed of coals.

Apple Sauce

It's a funny thing about apple sauce—the effort to peel the apples is what puts most people off making their own, and yet if you are dealing with unsprayed and unwaxed apples, you don't have to peel at all. Chewing will be required, but the teeth don't object to that. Cut up good, yellow or even green cooking apples, removing any blemishes or bad spots. Trace any worm to his lair, and ask him to leave. You need 4-5 apples per large serving of apple sauce, and may want to make extra for guests or keeping back for midnight raids on the icebox. Macrobiotic cooking asks that no sugar be used, but that's a matter for you to decide. Certainly a little honey or brown sugar is the idea, not cupfuls. Apples 'ain't' supposed to be candies. Chop apples and add to little water, honey and spice in pan over low heat, and cook until mushy. The sauce can also be added to: blackberries, blueberries, pineapple chunks, the apricot, and even the gooseberry. Spices are for you to enjoy: the usual cinnamon and cloves can be put aside for mace, allspice, nutmeg or even paprika.

Apple Tart Glorioso

Or as the punster I know wants to know, gloriosa? Don't know. What is known, is that punsters and all will quieten down if you come from the kitchen bearing this morsel of conviviality.

Using a pastry shell (p51) or making a crumb recipe using digestive biscuits (p92) is the place to start. Cut up enough cooking apples to fill a shell to overflowing. The apples should then be dusted with clove, cardamom, and a bit of lemon juice should be squeezed on. As the apples are in the shell only to be measured, remove and put in a bowl to spice. Next deseed 1 cup of white grapes, or dark purple ones if you can't find the seedless variety. Cut in halves, and put in the bowl with the apple. Allow to stand (the lemon will keep the apples from turning brown) for a few minutes. Then turn the bowl of fruit into a saucepan and gently cook the apples in the grapejuice without adding any water. This requires constant watching and turning for only about 5-8 min, as we are not out to make an applesauce, just to warm and steam the fruit. Remove from the heat, and cut in half a round of camembert cheese (minus the rind if you don't like its strong taste). Allow the cheese to melt. Turn the whole pan into the waiting shell, and slip into a moderate (350°F, 180°C, mark 4) oven. An apple cut into wedges may be used to decorate the tart, and must be cooked with it. Serve.

COOKED FRUITS

Do not overdo the cooking, or cook every fruit, as some lose food values with the presence of heat. A few have to be cooked to be edible, such as **rhubarb.** Check food value charts to be sure about the effects. **Dried apricots** and **prunes** have respectively 3·6mg Carotene (vitamin A) and 1mg if uncooked; and 1·2mg and ·50mg Carotene after cooking. The loss in nicotinic acid is similar. **Pears** seem to lose nothing nor **apples,** but then they are not so rich in vitamins as in minerals. **Currants** suffer a 30 per cent loss of vitamin C, though gram for gram they are still 3 times as rich in C than oranges. You will note that we leave our **strawberries** uncooked by way of preserving their large amount of vitamin C. If you drink the liquids as well, the best way to soften **dried apricots** is to leave them in warm water overnight. Then the loss is minimal. **Dried peaches** and **prunes** are particularly rich in minerals such as potassium and iron as are **dried currants** and **apricots.**

Grapefruit and Oranges

Can be cut in half, coated in honey or grape juice and grilled for morning warmth. The honey protects the C.

Cranberries

Are best looked over for bruises before cooking, and then cooked in the smallest amount of water until they pop. Sweeten with molasses or honey. **Gooseberries** can be cooked in the same manner.

Pears under Brie

Pears are the autumn equivalent of all those summer delights, such as strawberries or wild raspberries. They are, that is, if they are allowed to serve the function of not only good eating, but elegance. Cut nicely yellowed King Williams into quarters, and core out the seeds. Cover the cavity with thick slices of fresh Brie or, if you like the goatsmilk chevres, perhaps a St Marcellin. Grill lightly. Fast and provocative.

Pears Deluxe

Cut fresh coconuts into halves with a small saw. Square off the bottoms to make them sit up like cups. Using a sharp knife, cut the 'meat' away from the shell. Mix the coconut with cubes of fresh pear, bits of pineapple, jack fruit, berries, or seedless grapes. Grind liberal amounts of fresh nutmeg over the fruit, and spoon back into the shells. Top with rounds of Camembert, and grill until cheese is melted. Be sure not to let the fibres on the shell catch fire. Garnish with walnut halves.

Les Doigts D'Ananas aux Doigts

These are, if you want it in English, fingers of pineapple eaten with the fingers. Simply cut the pineapple from top to bottom 8-12 times to make long sections—as shown below. Serve with a candle in the top, and congratulate yourself on having avoided the messy cutting off of the rind. Besides, it's perfectly correct as it is perfectly Hawaiian. (*Note:* pineapples should be predominantly golden brown on the outside, and one of the leaves should pull out easily when it is ripe.)

Flaming Pineapple

If you have the patience, you can peel the pineapple, and then cut it into cubes. Sprinkle on a bit of raw dark brown sugar, or spread on one of the more exotic honeys, such as cactus or citrus blossom. Grill for a moment until the pineapple is thoroughly warmed and the sweetener melted in. Remove from heat and garnish with 'roses' made from whipped double cream piped on with a pastry tube. If your views on alcohol allow you to use a bit in cooking, pour a brandy over the cubes, and set on fire at serving time. For all the fun, and pure pineapple, merely soak the leaves in brandy, and fire them. Spectacular in a dark room for a party.

Apricots Royale

Sun ripened, slightly freckled apricots are dessert delight enough just in themselves. But sometimes while knowing that Nature cannot be improved upon, it is possible to alter the presentation. You can use peaches as well for this dish or nectarines, or all three can be mixed. The procedure is simple: cut open 5 or more apricots per serving and remove the seed. Place the apricot halves pitted side up on a baking sheet and sprinkle with powder cloves and dashes of cardamom. Place dollops of cream cheese or spoonfuls of yogurt in each pit. Grate a few almonds over the top of each, and place one almond (or other nut) in the centre of each apricot. Place under a hot grill for just minutes, until apricot juices appear, and the cheese is just a bit bubbly. Serve at once, and be prepared to be coaxed (ordered) back into the kitchen to do just a few more.

Rotegrot

This Scandinavian (more particularly Danish) delight is a sweet that none need apologize for eating. It needn't even be sweet if the berries and cherries are. What is needed initially is patience.

Stone 1lb (500g) Bing or black cherries— there is an instrument sometimes found in antique stores called a cherry stoner which punches the stone out—and clean 1lb (500g) raspberries or similar berry (*not* strawberries). Put fruit in a pan and add just enough water to cover the bottom. Cook until the simmering stage is reached, and watch carefully. The fruit should produce some liquid if not allowed to boil off. After the fruit is lightly cooked (just a few min), drain the liquid off into a measuring cup—it should make 1pt (570ml, $2\frac{1}{2}$ cups) of liquid; if not add hot water until the measure is reached. Heat liquid until almost boiling (when it steams and almost gurgles), and stir in a cream made from 1 heaped tsp of cornflour blended into 2 tbsp cold water. Turn heat down, and let the two liquids thicken. Then add the fruit, and allow all to cool in a bowl. If too sour for your taste serve with honey and cream.

NUTS

Nuts are the super seeds of the vegetarian world. They are the finest source of thiamine and are concentrated protein as a glance at the chart on p63 shows. Wet or unripe **walnuts** even have 1300-3000mg/100g of ascorbic acid or 500 times the daily requirement of vitamin C! But nuts must be treated with care, as the roasting of **peanuts** will cause them to lose 75 per cent of their .90mg of thiamine. Rancidity is nearly always a sign that too much heat and time has passed by, and the nut is no longer tasty because it is no longer good. You will find that we have been sprinkling nuts all the way through this book from the fruit and nut soups (p21) and the date and Brazil nut (80 per cent daily requirement of thiamine) hors d'oeuvre to the Banana and Nut Risotto on p70. But do read about them in a nutrition handbook and learn to use them instead of pills for getting in your vitamins. (They become quite economical if you buy in bulk from the growers, or even if you just wait for the after Christmas sales.) Do remember pistachios, cob nuts, pecans, chestnuts, hickory nuts, litchi nuts, macadamia nuts, torreya nuts and even water chestnuts.

To gain the most from nuts, the tough fibres have to be thoroughly chewed. Try, as an experiment, chewing a **Brazil nut** for 2 min. Then 3 or 4 min. Still, in any bulk, you may want to help the process mechanically, and for this a nut grinder, a chopper attachment to the blender, or a good knife and patience, are indispensible. Finely ground **almonds** mixed with a small amount of honey, and then put into the freezer for 15 min make the best kind of eggless marzipan. Or:

Fortune Tea

Grind almonds and hazelnuts (filberts) and add 4-6 tsp to each teacup of hot milk, along with a dash of cardamom and a sprinkle of ground nutmeg. Just the finale for a Chinese dinner. Or with a few cut up Brazil nuts, and almond pieces, a good mid-morning pick-you-up.

Homemade Nut Butters

Use the blender to make your own peanut, cashew, walnut or filbert butter. You may need to add small amounts of nut oils to get the accustomed texture. Wonderful spread on slices of whole wheat bread with handfuls of bean sprouts or cress.

Nutburgers and Nutloaves

Any prolonged cooking is not good for nuts, so discard any recipes that ask you to bake for hours. Simply mix whole wheat bread crumbs in a 1 to 1 proportion with ground nuts, adding a bit of hot milk for moisture. Make patties and fry for just a minute in a light vegetable oil. Or bake for just 10 min in a loaf tin, adding celery leaves for taste, and grated carrots for texture.

WEST COUNTRY RECIPES

Devonshire Hills Scones

Or, if you prefer to keep it all perfectly straight, Brown Splits.

Sift together:

1 lb (500g, 3 cups) self-raising whole wheat flour
1 tsp sea salt
2oz (60g) soft brown sugar

Cut or rub in 4oz (125g) butter until crumbly mixture is formed. Add ½pt (285ml, 1¼ cups) whole milk and make a soft dough. Roll out until about ½in (1cm) thick, and cut into circles with a metal cutter (or small glass). Bake on an oiled or teflon baking sheet for 8-10 min, 375°F (190°C, mark 5).

Serve slightly warm with that famous Devonshire Cream (which is technically a cheese) or fresh whipped cream, and some homemade jam made with honey (such as rosehip or our apple butter p 87 and p 78). But only occasionally.

Eva's Cornish Saffron Cake

3lb (1½kg, 12 cups) white unbleached flour
12oz (375g, 2 cups) brown sugar
12oz (375g) fat (vegetable shortening)—not lard
1-1½lb (500-750g, 4 cups) mixed dried fruit
orange and lemon peel
1drm ($\frac{1}{16}$oz) saffron which has boiled in
1pt (570ml, 2½ cups) water for 3 hours, or
preferably overnight
2oz (60g) fresh yeast or 1oz (30g) dried yeast

Cut the vegetable shortening into the flour and sugar until crumbly mixture is formed. Make a well in the mixture and add saffron water to make a dough. Stir in fruit and peel, and turn in yeast. (If dried yeast make up with warm saffron water.) The dough will be fairly dry.

Bake in moderate oven, 350°F (180°C, mark 4) for 30-45 min. The cake is a most beautiful yellow, and will carry you right out to Land's End. Eat in moderation if you can.

Teddy Pasty

In country Devon, there are still a few wonderful souls who know about and make pasties that originated in the rough days of subsistence farming. They were filling then and they still are.

Using the brown flour pastry on p 51, fill a tart tin, or roll out in a circle and fold over to make the half-moon shape. Put in slices of parboiled new potato (the richest in vitamin C, and other goodies) and spread with a thick layer of cream. Season with salt and pepper, and such herbs as you like (tarragon, basil or lovage). Bake until set for a few minutes in a hot oven, 400°F (200°C, mark 6), or longer in a cooler oven if the potatoes need it. Parboiled turnips can be used in the place of potatoes, or you can make alternate layers of each.

Autumn Apples

The apples of Devonshire and Somerset—or anywhere else for that matter—don't mind at all (there's an assumption for you) being neatly sliced crossways and then fried ever so gently in a bit of butter. Sprinkle on cloves and perhaps a dash of cardamom. You can dip them in a batter of whole wheat flour before frying as per the recipe on p 87.

Strawberry Pies

Collect enough strawberries, perhaps wild ones, to fill a good whole wheat pastry shell (p 51). The strawberries can be put whole and un-cooked into the shell and simply covered with cream. Or you can make a cream filling from the juice of a few crushed berries and a bit of corn flour (1-1½ tsp) per 8 fl oz (230ml, 1 cup) of liquid. Strawberries whipped into a cream cheese are the easiest of fillings, but they must not be allowed to stand about and get brown and mushy. Finally a packet of gelatine (or see our homemade on p 24) dissolved, with a bit of double cream coursed through, and poured when almost set upon the berries, will make a cool pleasure for the late afternoon tea time.

FOUND FOODS

ROSEHIPS

There is no need to regret the last roses of summer if you know that the bright orange-red berries which appear where the roses were— the hips—are as happy an occasion as were the first roses of the previous spring. Quite aside from their cheery beauty, they possess huge amounts of vitamin C (20 times that of oranges or even more). They can be eaten as found (washed, and in some cases, defuzzed). Some large ones, as a friend and I found in Norway, are as good as most plums. Or they can be carefully gathered (don't forget your gloves, some roses are a bit poisonous), sliced into quarters, and dried on cheese cloth in the sun. This gives you the 'makings' for winter teas. Other uses are for jellies as on the next page, or in apple butter, or in homemade marmalades. Use as decoration in autumn salads, or to brighten vegetables. Add at the last minute to preserve the vitamin content.

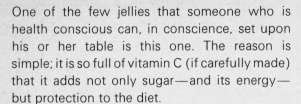

Rose Hip Jelly

One of the few jellies that someone who is health conscious can, in conscience, set upon his or her table is this one. The reason is simple; it is so full of vitamin C (if carefully made) that it adds not only sugar—and its energy—but protection to the diet.

Pick the ripe firm hips and simmer in enough water to cover. Don't boil. This process should go on until the hips are soft, anywhere from half an hour onwards—the time depends on the variety of rose hip, some of the really large ones can be done in 15 min! Then blend, or put through a sieve, and finally strain through a fine muslin or gauze cloth to capture any pieces of fuzzy skin. For every 1pt (570ml, $2\frac{1}{2}$ cups) of rose hip liquor add 1lb (500g, $2\frac{1}{4}$ cups) of brown sugar and the juice of a lemon, lime or orange (or blackcurrant juice, etc). Simmer again until jelly will form when liquid is dropped on a cold saucer. Seal into small jars. It's bread time.

COMFREY

The Germans living in my grandparents' areas of Iowa have always had great delight in traditional dishes, and a fine notion of natural herbery. One of their favourites is the comfrey plant which is just as widely and wildly found in Iowa as on the plains of Germany (and easily in backyards anywhere). The leaves are gathered and dried, and used infused as a tea for tonic purposes, though some use it with lemon and honey as a cooler for those hot 40°C days that plague the Mississippi River Valley in July. In combination with the Indian maize that is used to make corn bread (see p58) and polenta, a new use was obtained:

Comfrey Fritters

Make a batter of 2oz (60g) maize or corn meal, 2oz (60g) whole wheat flour, and enough milk to make a thin consistency. Spice with allspice. Dip the comfrey leaves in some milk (which is best chilled) then in the batter, and fry in several inches of light vegetable oil in a wok or a deep fry. Frying time should be for just seconds —when the batter goes light brown. Serve at once. Apples or pears, cut into rings, are the obvious sweet for comfrey, and they can be frittered as well.

Note: Fresh young comfrey leaves can be used in salads and are one of the best tasting sources of B_{12} in the vegetarian diet (they are even essential for vegans).

MINT

Fresh mint is about for the gathering in all sorts of places, or can be grown in a pot under the dripping water tap. In either case, you may have more of it than can be used, and one way to preserve it is to make:

Mint Syrup

Simmer several large handfuls into just a bit of water for $\frac{1}{2}$ hour, making sure the pan is air tight or else the house will be minty and the water vapid. Then strain through a sieve or fine cloth, and measure. For each 8 fl oz (230ml, 1 cup) of mint water, add about 10 tbsp of brown sugar, or 8 tbsp of honey. The juice of a lemon can be added, along with a bit of grated peel. Keep in fridge in a tight jar. Use to add zest to cool drinks such as lemonade, tea, apple juice, or in cooking.

FERN FRONDS

Fern fronds are those delightful bull-fiddle shaped growths which come up each spring or even late in the summer. In some dark and dense forest areas they continue to appear all year. They are edible raw as a salad when young, but when still uncurled may be lightly steamed in a basket (or bamboo tray) set over boiling water. If boiled they lose their delicate woodsy flavour. They are rich in chlorophyll and trace elements. Leave some when picking, as you do with wild mushrooms.

DANDELIONS

If you can't think of eating weeds such as dandelion in English, think of it as a French delicacy called Dent de Lion (lion's tooth) and know that it is a member of the chicory family. Or so my friend Myr said to my friend David by way of agreeing that this most common of flowers is a gourmet dish. As a salad, eat cold, and choose only the most tender leaves. Serve with croutons tossed in, and a good dressing. As a green, cook the small to medium leaves ever so gently with a dash of dill and some olive oil. And chew. Now wasn't Emily Dickinson right when she said that if the dandelion weren't so common we should value it as we do rare orchids? Just to prove the relationship to chicory, by the by, try ground dried dandelion roots as a herbal coffee. Richest of all greens in iron and trace elements.

FLOWERS

The Chinese use chrysanthemum petals to flavour sweets, the Indians use roses. Nasturtium buds oiled and salted become capers, and in North Devon and Wales Laver seaweed's buds are the greatest delicacy. Or dandelion flowers in the pastry . . . a few violets on the fresh fruit.

MUSHROOMS

Wild or domesticated, the mushroom is, until fried completely, low calory and one of the best diet items for watching the waistline. You can eat them raw, provided of course, you know something about their flavours. The wild ones must be eaten with great care in the raw state as some are only non-poisonous if they are cooked. The mushroom fried in oil takes on not only the smooth appearance which one is accustomed to, but also the calories contained in the oil. For this reason it is usually best to fry them in safflower oil or in a light olive oil. They can be served fried with green pepper or cheese just as an appetiser or on toast as a light snack.

Stuffed Mushrooms

The stuffed caps of mushrooms shown in the illustration above are a mini version of a mushroom casserole. They are prepared strictly by the whim of the mushroom spirit deciding to market those extra large caps, unless you know the friendly mushroom man. It is best to boil the caps for a moment before stuffing. They can be stuffed with peppers and cheese— Camembert if you are rolling in money and Cheshire if you are not. Turn out the stuffed caps onto toasted brown bread, and if you want something to go with the tops, make a little bit thicker than usual tomato sauce. Rice, nut meats and grains can also be used for stuffing.

THINGS TO DO

Pimentos

Here's your chance to create havoc. Get the large red, sweet peppers and put them under the grill, turn up the heat, and burn them. Turn over and burn the other side. Black. Oh happy day! Or hold over an open fire on toasting forks and burn. All to an end, for by burning the hard outer shell, and cooking the inside a bit, you are transforming peppers into pimentos. With a bowl of cool water by your side, remove the blackened skin as soon as you remove from the heat. Save the ash though, it's great for giving gravies and stews that outdoors' flavour. When the peppers are cool, cut into long slices. Keep in corner of the icebox until you are ready to use.

FRENCHIFICATORS

Beurre Noisette

Butter (un-salted) cooked over a low heat until it froths and turns nut-brown is perfect for any plain pasta and cheese dish, or on green vegetables. Add a squeeze of the garlic press—just the snap that makes whole wheat bread into garlic bread. Don't let it scorch.

Duxelles

Fry 1oz (30g) chopped shallots with 8oz (250g) of fried mushroom bits in a little olive oil and use to garnish rice, stuff tomatoes, or perk up a soup made of last night's leftovers.

Julienne

Stew thin slices of orange peel, lemon skin, whole slices of lime, paper-thin slices of cumquats, in just drops of water, spiced with powdered cloves and cardamom, until the water goes. Set aside on an open plate and let dry. Keep in fridge for sauces with fruit, cake icings, and for the odd cup of tea.

More Flowers

Nasturtiums in your salads; marigold leaves to decorate the white cheese; geranium leaves added to a jar of sugar and sealed to create new flavours; anemones on cheese cake; beauty for the thinking.

YOGURT

This is a food rich in the B-complex family, and calcium. Some varieties have extra friendly lactic bacteria that help the lower digestive tract to keep busy with its essential work. You probably know how to make yogurt, but in case you haven't made it in a while, or are a bit of a neophyte, here goes. I say here goes, because once you start, you'll probably be handing the culture on to your descendants; and here goes, because all sorts of weird things can happen. Should your yogurt ever begin to get a bit too sour, simply start all over again with a new culture. For each qt (1·2l, 5 cups) of milk, put in 3 tbsp of unflavoured yogurt from a friend, or the dry yogurt culture that you get at health food shops. Heat the milk in a heavy pan on a low heat. Don't let the milk boil, but do bring to the vapours steaming stage. Remove, and let cool to the point where you can put your finger in, but not leave it without getting signals from your head that it's too hot. Try to learn when you can hold out for about 15 sec. Add the yogurt or the culture, and put in jars which you then cover. Keep warm by setting the jars in a pan of 100°F (39°C) water with a good cover, or a 'yogurt-maker'. Keep the water warm on a radiator, or keep changing it. If you have gas, the pilot light may be quite good enough. After 3 hours or more (even most of a day) the yogurt should gel, and the test is a knife inserted and cleanly removed. Refrigerate. Save some for next time. Do your own toppings.

YOGURT TOPPINGS

If you live in the country, you can simply take a walk, most of the year, and come back with all the toppings that yogurt can ever use: berries from the bushes, even in December; the reddest of apples cut into wedges; fresh mushrooms to steam fry lightly before using, various wild plants such as dandelion, fern fronds, and mint leaves (see p88), or just a few turnip leaves to cut into strips and steam. The point is that you never need eat another sugar sweetened topping. A town walk will net cumquats, or Yorkshire blueberries, or your aunt's homemade preserves, or a mango to slice, or green peppers. An acquaintance of ours brings a bowl of yogurt to work, with a sandwich of some variety, and then ventures out to see what new mixture he can find in one of the ethnic stores that abound in cities. He has a walk, meets new souls, adventures a bit, and enjoys his lunch. Beansprouts on Monday, fresh figs on Tuesday, loquats from a Chinese store, vine leaves from a Greek shop, and mandarin oranges for Friday. Or work a little. Since even the logicians of Gilbert and Sullivan could never figure out whether dill was invented for cucumbers or cucumbers for dill, combine them with a bit of tomato, a grind from the peppercorn grinder, and goatsmilk yogurt (if you can get it, and your own if you can't). Ah!

Lynn's Cream Cheese Cake

Regular cheese cake is usually full of eggs or chemicals, so summer's fresh fruits, or winter's frozen, deserve a better bed.

Crust: A crumb crust made of a tea cup of crushed digestive biscuits (graham crackers), or zweibach crumbs mixed with 4-6 tbsp melted butter, 4 tbsp dark brown sugar, and liberal dashes of cinnamon and nutmeg, mixed together and pressed into a deep round tin whose side collapses or opens (spring form). Chill until quite firm.

Filling: 8oz (250g, 1 cup) of brown sugar, and zests of grated lemon and orange peel (or a few cranberries) are fluffed and beaten into five 8oz (250g) packets of cream cheese. Sprinkle 3 tbsp of natural white flour and $\frac{1}{4}$ tsp salt all over if desired, and whip cheese some more. Then add the equivalent of 5 eggs: 5 tbsp arrowroot or soy flour with 2 tbsp water, 5 tbsp almond or cashew nut butter, or 5 tbsp lecithin. Finally for smoothness add 4 tbsp double cream. Pour filling into the crust, and bake at 500°F (260°C, mark 9) until mixture begins to brown, about 15 min. Then reduce to 250°F (120°C, mark $\frac{1}{4}$) for one hour. Remove and cool. Remove side of pan, and refrigerate until cold. Top with fresh strawberries, blueberries, pitted cherries, pineapple, in teacups full of the yogurt you made on p91!

JUICES

Folk on the natural diet sooner or later encounter one of the machines that is actually of use to man—the juicer. Good ones are expensive, and you may prefer to chew, as the teeth are superb grinders if used. The machine has the advantage of extracting the cellulose fibre, something that the vegetarian often has quite enough of. But I think the appeal of juicers is mainly aesthetic. The beauty of a glass of freshly-made carrot juice is only surpassed by its taste. If you do invest in a juicing machine, use it.

Use it to make carrot-and-apple juice for an addition to lunch; to make apricot-peach-cherry ambrosia (stone first) or to obtain Indian delights such as mango and papaya juices. Be careful about celery juice on its own as it can be overly salty, so mix it with tomatoes, parsley, lettuce, and carrots (and even quartered cucumber) for a liquid salad.
  Globe artichokes are obviously a no-no.

Commercial juices are often disappointing with the exception of apple and grape juices, the variety of which will amaze those friends of yours who live to drink the wine with which they dine. Your liver will appreciate your care.

A hand juicer can produce magic for the morning. An orange, a grapefruit, a lemon (or lime) can all be juiced together and served in warm water with a bit of blackcurrant to create culinary velvet. All of your daily vitamin C, and a system that is regular—these are the bonuses. Made with 1 tsp rose hip jelly (see p87), and you can most likely waltz past winter miseries.

Cranberry juice can be obtained from cooking a packet of berries over the lowest of heat, until the pulp is quite soft (time varies according to the thickness of the berry skin). Drain through a cheese cloth, and then squeeze the pulp that the cloth catches. Serve warm or chilled as a morning or evening 'cocktail'.

Bananas can be blended into milk for a shake, or coconut milk (made from soaking freshly grated coconut in water and then filtering and squeezing as with the cranberries) can be used to thin out a blender full of strawberries. Great for the mother-to-be, and useful in calming the father-to-be.

If you have no other use for the 'pot liquors' that remain from cooking green beans, or carrots, or beets, allow to cool and have as a mid-washing-up refresher course.

TEAS AND TISANES

Teas are a matter for you to decide, as they are bound to be tied to your own sense of what you want. But if one survey is correct, $5\frac{3}{4}$ cups a day is the full dose of caffeine and tannin permitted for health! Tannin is fixed if milk is used and, if the sugar content is watched, the natural fluorides in tea may in fact help prevent decay of teeth. Obviously you will want a good tea, and will spend the few extra pennies to avoid dyed and harsh teas.

Coffee is likewise a personal matter, but whereas a cup of tea may help you get ready for a morning meditation, coffee keeps many people in a restless state. Doctors are often confronted with nerves that are the result of 10 or more cups a day—so experiment with chicory, dandelion root beverage, postum, or one of the fig drinks. Some herbal coffees taste quite refreshing.

Hot water and lemon or lime with a bit of honey (if desired) has kept many regular for years, and with a bit of fresh mint is a good digestive.

Tisanes are various leaves and flowers used on the continent to perk up, relax, or give comfort to. Do try linden, camomile, verbena, anise, fresh mint or peppermint, and orange blossoms. Or learn from the American Indian and infuse sassafras roots, or boil up sarsparilla for a tea that can easily be drunk cold (root beer). Rose hip tea is discussed elsewhere (p86) as is comfrey, but lemon grass, raspberry leaves, sage, red clover flowers and leaves, the South American yerba mate or yerba sante, wild cherry bark, vervain, pennyroyal, nettles, lavender, the Cherokee golden seal, the Chinese Fo Ti Teng, and catnip are yours to enjoy and explore. We need liquids every day, and if they are warmed and pleasant, thus attracting the attention of the mind away from worries, tisanes are the obvious thing to do.

Don't neglect warmed apple and grape juices, which become tisanes when herbs and spices are added.

Bancha twig tea and Mu tea are macrobiotic contributions.

Adding an Indian spice mixture sold as marsala will add pungency to your tea; cardamom seeds (ground or whole) with a dash of allspice and just a touch of powdered clove will make a tea mixed with warm milk into the perfect digestive aid for an Indian dinner.

NUTRITION NOTES

Nutrition is a vast subject that we cannot cover in any adequate way other than to have provided recipes which reflect a conscious attempt to see that a vegetarian doesn't lack any essentials. Rose hips have been studied because they are 40 times richer than oranges in vitamin C. Sprouting seeds and beans are another high source, and the maligned potato has been given due credit. Proteins have been another concern, and I hope that the chart on p63 will silence any doubts about the food values of nuts, cheeses, and grains.

Some tips: If the cooking water is allowed to come to a boil first (especially when using herbal infusions) and the vegetables dropped right in, any enzyme action that might destroy the vitamins is minimized. Steam-frying protects vitamins as well. Most fruits and vegetables lose value while being stored, so try to use at once. This is especially true of new potatoes.

Food values are only averages. Good soil gives better values, and leached soil poorer values. Humans vary in the amount of certain nutrients required. Exercise increases the amount of energy needed and is the real controlling device for using up fat and carbohydrates (and excess protein), besides eating less. A check of the iron content in the blood, especially for women, is a good annual observation. Vegans must be careful of their B_{12} intake—some B_{12} pills are from micro-organisms and are therefore acceptable. Oatmeal loses 10 per cent of its thiamine content in cooking, puffy varieties of oats have none at all. Your lower intestine manufactures your B vitamins on the whole, and sitting or walking in even the winter sun will greatly enhance your vitamin D. Old carrots have 2000 micrograms of A. Watercress, figs, rhubarb and almonds are rich in calcium, lentils and almonds have higher riboflavine content. Seaweed for trace minerals, as well as greens from the woods, such as iron-rich dandelions. A middle-aged human doing little physical labour needs the following daily—vast excesses are just wasted money:

2800 calories (celery has almost none, lentils and nuts abundant).

60 grams of protein (balanced for amino acid content—beans, nuts and lentils are 25 per cent or more protein, grains 10 per cent).

5000 I.U. vitamin A (or 750 micrograms retinol equivalents) Dairy products, or their source, green leafy veggies such as spinach with 5 times the requirement.

400 I.U. vitamin D from milk or sunshine.

500mg calcium or a few oz of watercress.

10mg iron or haricot beans, or a few figs and some vitamin B such as in yeast.

FURTHER READING

The Composition of Foods, R. A. McCance and E. M. Widdowson, HMSO, London, 1960 (and revised editions)

The Composition of Foods, B. K. Watt and A. L. Merrill, US Dept of Agriculture Handbook No 8, Washington, 1963 (and revised editions)

Diet for a Small Planet, Franice Lappé, Friends of the Earth/Ballantine Press, NY, 1972

The Foods We Eat, ed Geoffrey Warren, Cassell, London, 1958

The Health Food Guide, Michael Balfour and Judy Alan, Garnstone Press, 59 Brompton Rd, London SW3, 1972 (gives mail order addresses, locates shops and cafes)

Herbs for all Seasons, Rosemary Hemphill, Angus and Robertson, Sydney and London, 1972

Vegetarian Recipes, Shilla A. Judd; Scientific Nutrition Book and Cookbook, Dona G. Kelly; The Wheel of Life, and other books, Kirpal Singh, all from Sant Bani Ashram, Franklin, New Hampshire, USA

Also good, but a bit heavy going, are the FAO (United Nations) nutrition guides, especially Protein Requirements, WHO technical report No 301, Rome, 1965, and various vegetarian magazines such as Seed, 8 All Saints Rd, London W11, and the journals of the Vegetarian and Vegan Societies.

INDEX